The All American
An Illustrated History of the 82nd Airborne Division

The All American

An Illustrated History of
the 82nd Airborne Division

1917 - to the Present

Robert P. Anzuoni

Schiffer Military History
Atglen, PA

Dedication
To my wife, and best friend, Sara,
And to all who served in the
All American Division.

Book design by Robert Biondi.

Copyright © 2001 by Robert P. Anzuoni.
Library of Congress Catalog Number: 2001090304.

Printed in China.
ISBN: 0-7643-1321-5

We are always looking for people to write books on new and related subjects. If you have an idea for a book, please contact us at the address below.

Published by Schiffer Publishing Ltd.
4880 Lower Valley Road
Atglen, PA 19310
Phone: (610) 593-1777
FAX: (610) 593-2002
E-mail: Schifferbk@aol.com.
Visit our web site at: www.schifferbooks.com
Please write for a free catalog.
This book may be purchased from the publisher.
Please include $3.95 postage.
Try your bookstore first.

In Europe, Schiffer books are distributed by:
Bushwood Books
6 Marksbury Ave.
Kew Gardens
Surrey TW9 4JF
England
Phone: 44 (0)208 392-8585
FAX: 44 (0)208 392-9876
E-mail: Bushwd@aol.com.
Free postage in the UK. Europe: air mail at cost.
Try your bookstore first.

Contents

Introduction

"The splendid esprit of the 82nd Airborne Division ... made it a command of which to be proud. Its combat record was second to none."
- General Omar N. Bradley

"This is a Division that is All-American, and as an American, I am proud of it."
- President John F. Kennedy

The 82nd Airborne Division is one of the most renowned fighting organizations in the world. The 82nd was the first airborne division of the United States and has been an active division since 1942. The 82nd helped develop the concepts of airborne warfare during World War II. After the war the 82nd continued to develop airborne techniques and trained to provide the United States with a strategic deployment force. Since World War II, the Division has been called upon to assist in domestic and foreign disturbances. Although the 82nd is an airborne division today, its origins are traced back to the 82nd Infantry Division of World War I. Since that time the Division has gone through many changes, but it still bears its World War I nickname: the "All American."

This history has been written to tell the story of the 82nd Airborne Division from its birth in 1917 to the present – the year 2000 saw the eighty-second anniversary of its entry into combat on the battlefields of western Europe during the First World War.

This book is a history of the Division itself through many changes from a World War I square division to the rapid deployment organization it is today, and uses many archival records. It is therefore concise, to allow the reader to easily get the big picture of what the 82nd has done and how it was organized to do its job. Many small operations are mentioned to give recognition to those who served. However, a division is a large organization that often has elements involved in several events at any one time. Only some training exercises have been mentioned because the 82nd trains constantly. Finally, only a few personal accounts of soldiers have been included where their experiences represent those of the Division. It is hoped that this history will serve the 82nd Airborne Division troopers of today as a reminder of their history and a tribute to our veterans.

chapter one

The 82nd Division, American Expeditionary Forces: World War I

When the United States entered World War I, it was woefully unprepared for the scale of warfare being waged in Europe. Even with the mobilization of the Regular Army and National Guard, the Army had only 200,000 troops. After inspecting the battlefields of Europe, General Pershing advised the War Department to raise a force of three million. Congress had already taken steps to increase the military with the Selective Service Act of May 1917, which established a system of conscription. The Selective Service Act also created the National Army which would provide the structure to organize and train the rapid influx of conscript troops.

As part of the National Army, the 82nd Division was organized on 25 August 1917 at Camp Gordon, Georgia, near Atlanta. The unit was commanded by Major General Eben Swift. Brigadier General James Erwin took command in November, but he was soon succeeded by Brigadier General William Burnham in December. The Division contained soldiers of many different ethnic backgrounds from all of the forty-eight states. A popular contest was held in Atlanta to give a name to the division instead of an impersonal number. Thousands of replies were received. In April 1918 the governor and General Burnham finally decided upon the name "All American" because it best described the members and spirit of the Division. On 1 August the 82nd adopted a red, white, and blue shoulder patch with the letters "AA" in the center. Both the nickname and the patch have been symbols of the 82nd since then.

The 82nd was organized as a square division which consisted of two infantry brigades, each containing two infantry regiments. There were also an artillery brigade and support troops. This structure gave the American divisions 28,000 men, nearly twice the amount of British, French, or German divisions. Although the square division was difficult to control, it afforded greater striking and staying power which would be needed to break the enemy defenses. The major units of the 82nd and the structure of a regiment are shown in *Table 1* (opposite).

While at Camp Gordon the 82nd trained for trench warfare. Small arms training was conducted at a range in Norcross and artillery training was conducted at Blackjack Mountain, both in Georgia. Because of supply shortages, much of the training utilized wooden guns. On 10 April 1918 the "All American" left Georgia and headed for New York. Brigadier General Burnham was promoted to Major General. After a brief stay, the Division embarked for England on the 25th, and lead elements arrived on 7 May.

Most of the troops proceeded to Southampton to embark for Le Havre, France. The 325th Infantry Regiment, however, passed through London and was reviewed by King George V of England, on 11 May 1918, marking the first time that an American unit was reviewed by British royalty. The event also gave the United States a chance to show its National Army to an Allied nation. The other Allied nations had been engaged in war for four years, and eagerly awaited the arrival of fresh American troops to turn the tide. The streets were lined with cheering crowds, and the king personally greeted the Regimental and Battalion commanders. The 325th's parade was significant because it demonstrated America's commitment to the Allies by providing well-trained troops.

Table 1

Table 1
THE 82nd DIVISION IN WORLD WAR I

Headquarters, 82nd Division

Divisional Troops	163rd Infantry Brigade	164th Infantry Brigade	157th Field Artillery
307th Engineer Regiment	325th Infantry Regiment	327th Infantry Regiment	319th Field Artillery Regiment
307th Field Signal Battalion	326th Infantry Regiment	328th Infantry Regiment	(155mm howitzers)
307th Sanitary Train	320th Machine Gun Battalion	321st Machine Gun Battalion	320th Field Artillery Regiment
307th Supply Train			(75mm gun)
307th Mobile Ordnance			321st Field Artillery Regiment
Repair Shop			(75mm gun)
319th Machine Gun Battalion			307th Trench Mortar Battery
82nd Military Police Company			(6" mortar)

Infantry Regiment
Headquarters and Headquarters Company

1st Battalion	2nd Battalion	3rd Battalion	Machine Gun Company	Supply Company
Headquarters	Headquarters	Headquarters		
HQ Company	HQ Company	HQ Company	**Medical Detachment**	
A Company	E Company	I Company		
B Company	F Company	K Company		
C Company	G Company	L Company		
D Company	H Company	M Company		

The Headquarters of the 82nd opened on 16 May in Escarbotin, Somme, France. The troops received British manufactured Lewis and Vickers machine guns, protective masks, and helmets because of the shortage of American equipment. An intensive training program was soon instituted. Weapons firing, bayonet drills, road marching, and instruction in trench warfare were part of the daily routine. On 30 May, General Pershing inspected the Division to check on its combat readiness. To gain experience, officers and non-commissioned officers of the 82nd visited British units in the front-line trenches. On 9 June 1918, Captain Henry Lee Jewett Williams of the 326th Infantry Regiment was killed during one of the tours, making him the first casualty of the Division. Captain Williams was typical of the high caliber soldiers of the 82nd. He held two degrees from Oxford and was an Episcopal priest. Before joining the Army, he was a professor of Greek. When offered a commission as a chap-

lain, he insisted on being infantry. When he was severely wounded, he told a non-commissioned officer, "I am fine" then instructed him to check on another wounded soldier. Captain Williams was evacuated, but died later that evening from his wounds.

On 16 June, the Division moved by train to Toul. Since the 82nd had moved into a French sector, British weapons were turned in and the troops received French Chauchat automatic rifles and Hotchkiss 8mm machine guns. By using French weapons, resupply would be made easier. The Division's assignment was to relieve the 26th Division in the Lagny Sector near the city of Toul in northeastern France. That section of the western front was known as the Woëvre Front. The mission was conducted on 25 June. Although the area was considered a defensive sector, the 82nd actively patrolled and conducted raids. The first large scale raid of the Division occurred on 4 August when Companies K and M of the 326th Infantry Regiment, supported by the 320th Machine Gun Battalion, attacked German positions and penetrated over 600 meters into enemy lines. The raid was small compared to the operations the Division would soon conduct, but it provided valuable experience. On 10 August, the 82nd was relieved by the 89th Division, and moved to the area west of Toul.

The 82nd was ordered to relieve the 2nd Division in the Marbache Sector on 15 August. The Division trained in this area until 11 September. On the 12th, the Division was committed to the St. Mihiel Offensive. After completing its mission the 82nd was once again stationed in the Marbache Sector from 17-20 September. On the 20th, the Division was relieved at the front and moved to Marbache to prepare for the Meuse-Argonne Offensive, ending its participation in the Lorraine Campaign.

The Allies were planning two large offensive operations for the fall of 1918 that would reduce German pockets of resistance known as salients. One of these was the St. Mihiel salient, which was traingular in shape. The angles of this salient were located near Verdun, St. Mihiel, and Pont-a-Mousson. The St. Mihiel salient penetrated almost twenty-five kilometers into allied lines and severed the Verdun-Toul railroad. From positions in the salient, the Germans were able to disrupt traffic on the Paris-Nancy railroad. Since troop transportation and resupply depended heavily upon railroads, control of key rail systems was important for conducting and sustaining large operations. Any operation in the Meuse-Argonne region would be threatened by positions in the St. Mihiel salient. The French had been trying to dislodge the Germans from the salient since 1914, but they had been unsuccessful. It was hoped that the arrival of the American divisions would turn the tide.

To reduce the St. Mihiel salient, the American First Army was formed with the I, IV, and V Corps. Sixteen American divisions, augmented by the French II Colonial Corps, were available for the attack – a total of 665,000 troops. The 82nd was assigned to the I Corps, and was placed on the far right flank on the south side of the salient. Its original mission was to make contact and keep pressure on the enemy.

On 12 September the First Army began its attack on the St. Mihiel salient. The 82nd sent out patrols along the east bank of the Moselle River, but the main thrust of the Division was on the west bank heading north to Norroy.

The 82nd's advance also covered the right flank of the 90th Division. Throughout the 14th, German artillery shelled the area with high explosive rounds and mustard gas, but the 82nd held. On the 15th, the 82nd continued the attack, entering Vandieres and securing Hill 218 to the north. Heavy casualties were caused by enemy artillery. During this attack, Colonel Emory Pike, Division Machine Gun Officer, was wounded, and later died. For his actions, he was cited by the Division and later was awarded the Medal of Honor, making him the first member of the 82nd to earn the nation's highest military decoration. The 82nd was relieved on 21 September, ending the first major offensive of the Division.

The second large scale offensive planned by the Allies would reduce the German salient in the Argonne Forest and Meuse River valley. The key objective, however, was the Carigan-Sedan-Mezieres railroad, which was a vital German supply line. Dislodging the Germans proved to be a difficult task because they had constructed a series of three defensive lines. The last line consisted of a series of hills, ridges, woods, trenches, and barbed wire that was known as the Kriemhilde Stellung. The position was the last defense before the railroad, which was vital to supply the German Army in the Meuse-Argonne region. Part of the 82nd's mission would be to breach the Kriemhilde Stellung.

The I Corps began its attack in the Argonne on 25 September while the 82nd was held in reserve. On 4 October, Major General George Duncan assumed command of the Division. Some elements of the Division were used to assist the 28th and 35th Divisions. On 6 October, the 82nd was ordered to clear the east edge of the Argonne to relieve pressure on the 1st Division which had been receiving fire from that area. LtC. Buxton, Division historian stated:

"In selecting the 82nd Division to perform this thrust into the flanks of the Argonne Forest, the 1st Corps had honored this Division with a heavy share of its expressed mission toward which it had been bending every resource for eleven terrible days."

On the 7th, the 164th Brigade crossed the Aire River to the west bank and seized its first two objectives – Hill 180 and Hill 223. For the next two days the battle raged back and forth as the Americans attacked and the Ger-

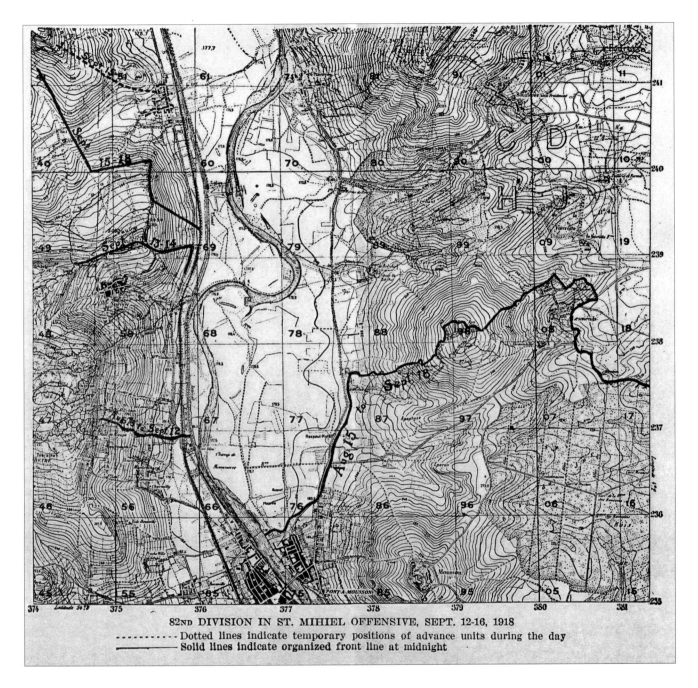

82ND DIVISION IN ST. MIHIEL OFFENSIVE, SEPT. 12-16, 1918
- - - - - - - - - - Dotted lines indicate temporary positions of advance units during the day
————————— Solid lines indicate organized front line at midnight

mans counter-attacked. On 8 October, a detachment of fifteen men was sent to secure a hill on which there were almost 250 enemy troops of a German machine gun battalion. Corporal Alvin York, leading several soldiers, captured 132 prisoners and 35 machine guns. For his action, York was personally congratulated by General Pershing, and also received the Medal of Honor and the French Croix de Guerre. On 10 October, the 163rd Brigade joined the 164th. By the end of the day the Division held Cornay, the high ground to the north, a portion of the Decauville Railroad, and had cleared the eastern half of the Argonne.

Typical of the bravery of an "All American" soldier in the early phase of the Meuse-Argonne was Sergeant Ernest S. Jones of F Company, 328th Infantry. On 10 October, his diary entry reads, "Am slightly gassed. Go to first aid station and rejoin company." A citation from the Division Commander gives a clearer picture of the reality Sgt. Jones faced:

While his battalion was making an attack, Sgt. Jones was struck by the explosion of an enemy gas shell and rendered unconscious. Altho [sic] suffering severely from the effects of the gas he refused to be evacuated and remained with his platoon, rendering valuable service in the reorganizing of it, which duty he performed under heavy artillery and machine gun fire and with entire disregard of his personal safety.

The second phase of the 82nd's operation called for the Division to fight astride the Aire River. The 326th, on the west bank, attacked north to St. Juvin. The 325th, 327th, and 328th, on the east bank, attacked north to the ridge that lies southeast of St. Juvin in order to breach the Kriemhilde Stellung. All objectives were gained and defended against counter-attacks. The 82nd had won a foothold in the Kriemhilde Stellung.

The Division continued its attack northward on the 14th. On that day the 82nd and 77th captured St. Juvin. The next day, German troops launched a counter-attack

which caused heavy casualties within the Division. Many casualties came from enemy guns on Hill 182 to the north of town. It became evident that the capture of the hill was necessary to hold St. Juvin and the surrounding area. Captain Frank Williams of MG Company, 325th Infantry, was assigned the task of securing Hill 182. Personally leading his troops, Williams cleared the hill, allowing the 82nd to continue its advance.

For the next few days the 82nd was involved in fighting in the Agron River Valley and the Ravin aux Pierres. By the 21st of October, the Division had the valley and the ravine in its possession. The following several days found the Division conducting routine patrols. The Division also maintained outposts to deny the enemy any knowledge of the buildup of fresh troops and ammunition for the final assault. On 1 November, the 82nd was relieved by the 77th and 80th Divisions. The 82nd proceeded to training areas in the rear to rest and train. On

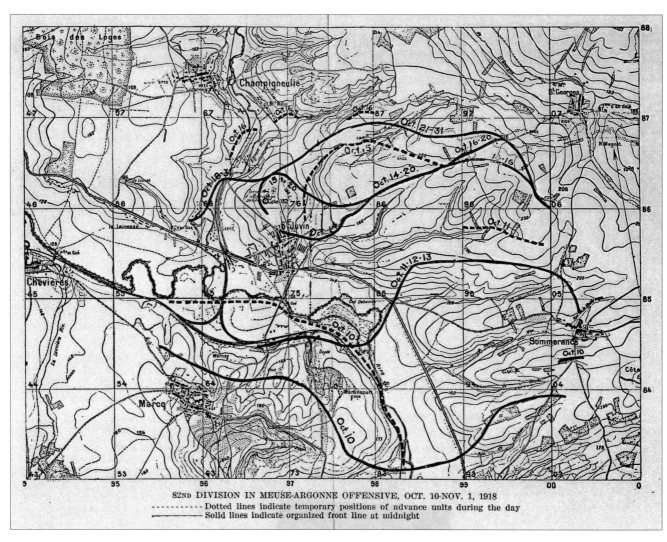

82ND DIVISION IN MEUSE-ARGONNE OFFENSIVE, OCT. 10-NOV. 1, 1918
- - - - - - - - - - Dotted lines indicate temporary positions of advance units during the day
——————— Solid lines indicate organized front line at midnight

11 November 1918, an armistice was signed, bringing an end to hostilities. In April 1919, units started to return to the United States. By June the last troops of the Division had returned and the 82nd was demobilized.

During its brief career the 82nd Division participated in some of the fiercest fighting of the largest campaigns. In the St. Mihiel Offensive the Division casualties numbered over 800 and over 6,000 in the Meuse-Argonne. In all, the 82nd suffered more than 7,000 casualties, including over 1,000 killed, during service in the First World War.

The Division also made contributions to the science of war. These included an improved method of effectively employing weapons and a system for coordinating machine gun and artillery fire. American divisions did not lack fire-power, but trying to orchestrate a large number of different weapons so as to attain the maximum effect was a problem. Many of the weapons, such as the 37mm gun and the Chauchat, were new. The 82nd coordinated the fire of its artillery and machine guns on map overlays to ensure that key terrain and enemy positions were covered. Such planning led to more effective destruction of enemy positions, and the system was adopted by other units.

The 82nd Division: Organized Reserves (1921-1942)

A little known period of 82nd history is the time between the World Wars. The Division was not involved in any major events, but it did serve as a part of the Organized Reserves. The 82nd had been demobilized on 27 May 1919 at Camp Mills, New York, after returning from overseas. The Division was reconstituted, i.e., restored to the official rolls of the Army, on 24 June 1921. Headquarters of the 82nd Division assembled at Columbia, South Carolina, on 23 September 1921. Elements of the Division were located in South Carolina, Georgia, and Florida. The regiments conducted two weeks of annual training in a variety of locations, often with active duty troops. Training was frequently hampered by supply shortages and a lack of funds. Artillery units traveled to Fort Bragg, North Carolina, which was an army artillery center. The soldiers of the 82nd Division did not know that one day Fort Bragg would become home to the 82nd Airborne Division.

The shoulder sleeve insignia of the 82nd Division – The All American.

Souvenir Program of the 325th march through London, 11 May 1918.

Rifle marksmanship training at Camp Gordon, Georgia, 1917.

Artillerymen of B Battery, 320th Artillery, training in Marietta, Georgia, April 1918.

Soldiers of the 320th Machine Gun Battalion training with a Lewis light machine gun at Camp Gordon, Georgia, 1917.

The 325th Infantry Regiment parades through London, England, 11 May 1918.

A squad of 307th Engineers supports a raid of the 326th Infantry on 4 August 1918 at Flirey, France.

SGT Ernest S. Jones of F Company, 328th Infantry in France, 1918 – An All American Soldier.

SGT Alvin C. York at Hill 223 near Chatel-Chehery, France, January 1919. This was the scene of his action in October 1918.

Opposite: Division Headquarters in Prauthoy, France, 17 January 1919.

SGT George A. Hoch of D Company, 320th Machine Gun Battalion in France, 1918.

ALL AMERICAN
BULLETIN

SOUTH CAROLINA   GEORGIA   FLORIDA

EIGHTY-SECOND DIVISION
COLUMBIA, S. C.

PUBLISHED IN THE INTEREST OF NATIONAL DEFENSE

Cover of the ALL AMERICAN BULLETIN, vol. 1, No. 5 October 1925. This was a professional publication of the 82nd Division, Organized Reserves.

The 325th Infantry Regiment, 82nd Division, Organized Reserves, receiving WWI campaign streamers from Colonel Wilder in August 1932.

chapter two

The 82nd Airborne Division:
World War II

Japan's sudden attack on U.S. military facilities at Pearl Harbor, Hawaii, found the United States unprepared for war. The attack greatly accelerated the military build-up underway since 1940. With rapid mobilization came the activation of many reserve divisions. On 25 March 1942, the 82nd Division was called to active duty. The 82nd was to be manned by 16,000 drafted soldiers and a nucleus of 2,000 experienced soldiers from the 9th Division. Major General Omar Bradley was appointed the commander with Brigadier General Matthew B. Ridgway as his Assistant Division Commander, and Brigadier General Joseph Swing as the Division Artillery Commander.

The 82nd Division was organized at Camp Claiborne, Louisiana, as a triangular infantry division which was built around three infantry regiments. This structure allowed for two regiments on the front line and one in reserve, hence the title "triangular." The 82nd Division units of 1942 are listed in *Table 2* on page 22.

General Bradley decided to introduce a system that would allow the effective processing of the new troops. He believed that it would create high morale and an efficient fighting force. Recruits were greeted at a reception station and interviewed. They were then assigned to positions based on their civilian skills, e.g., cooks became Army cooks, and truck drivers became Army truck drivers. In addition, leaders were carefully selected. The Division also conducted special training to create a cohesive fighting force. In order to promote esprit de corps, General Bradley reminded the troops of the World War I feats of the 82nd and invited Alvin York to visit the Division. York had become a folk hero after World War I, and

a 1941 movie about him, featuring Gary Cooper, made him even more popular. For the special occasion, a band was formed and a song – The All American Soldier – was written by Carl Sigman for the 82nd. The visit increased morale and provided another benefit. After York mentioned that he did his best shooting at short distance, a special close-range firing course was established with partially concealed targets. Repeated training on the course made the soldiers proficient in close combat fighting.

In June 1942, General Bradley was assigned to another division. Ridgway was promoted to Major General and assumed command of the 82nd. The following month, the Army decided to form a motorized division for the rapid movements that were expected in modern warfare. The 82nd was chosen because of its high level of training. Trucks began arriving shortly, and the troops started training to be motorized infantry. The 82nd would be a pioneer division, but in another field. The 82nd would have the honor of being the first airborne division of the United States.

The U.S. Army decided to form airborne divisions because the Germans had successfully employed airborne troops in Norway, Holland, Belgium, and Crete. Once again, the 82nd was chosen because of its combat readiness, which was a tribute to the abilities of Generals Bradley and Ridgway. The Division was also located near an airfield in a part of the country that allowed airborne training to be conducted during most of the year. A nucleus of soldiers was drawn from the 82nd to create another airborne division – the 101st. The 82nd was reorganized and redesignated the 82nd Airborne Division on 15 August 1942. The new organization can be seen in *Table 3* (below):

On 1 October 1942, the 82nd moved to Fort Bragg, North Carolina, where training continued and the last major changes were made before deploying overseas. The 326th was withdrawn and the 505th PIR, commanded by Colonel James Gavin, was added. The 456th PFAB, the 782nd Airborne Ordnance Maintenance Company, and a provisional Parachute Maintenance Company were also added. Brigadier General Maxwell Taylor became Division Artillery (Divarty) Commander and Brigadier General Keerans became the Assistant Division Commander (ADC). The organization of the 82nd Airborne Division as it deployed to North Africa in 1943 is shown in *Table 4* (opposite). The 82nd continued its training at Fort Bragg,

and in March 1943 the Division was inspected by General Marshall and British Foreign Secretary Anthony Eden. A large scale parachute operation still had not been tried by U.S. airborne forces. It was necessary to practice such an operation before deploying the new formations in combat. On 29 March, Colonel Gavin led his 505th PIR on the first U.S. regimental assault. The main objective was a bridge over the Wateree River near Camden, South Carolina. A number of distinguished visitors, including Winston Churchill and General Marshall were gathered at the site. The exercise was successful, but, unfortunately three paratroopers were killed when they were stuck by an airplane which had lost power.

Having proved the success of large scale airborne operations, the 82nd was prepared to move overseas. In April the Division moved to Camp Edwards, Massachu-

---

Table 2
THE 82nd DIVISION, 1942

Headquarters, 82nd Division

Headquarters Company, 82nd Division

		Headquarters, 82nd Division Artillery
307th Engineer Battalion	325th Infantry Regiment	319th Field Artillery Battalion (105mm)
307th Medical Battalion	326th Infantry Regiment	320th Field Artillery Battalion (105mm)
407th Quartermaster Battalion	327th Infantry Regiment	321st Field Artillery Battalion (155mm)
82nd Reconnaissance Troop		907th Field Artillery Battalion (105mm)
82nd Signal Company		
82nd Military Police Platoon		

Table 3
THE 82nd AIRBORNE DIVISION, 1942

Headquarters, 82nd Airborne Division

Headquarters Company, 82nd Airborne Division

307th Airborne Engineer Battalion	325th Glider Infantry Regiment
80th Airborne Antiaircraft Battalion	326th Glider Infantry Regiment
307th Airborne Medical Company	504th Parachute Infantry Regiment
407th Airborne Quartermaster Company	
82nd Airborne Signal Company	**Headquarters, 82nd Airborne Division Artillery**
82nd Airborne Reconnaissance Platoon	319th Glider Field Artillery Battalion (75mm)
82nd Airborne Military Police Platoon	320th Glider Field Artillery Battalion (105mm)
	376th Parachute Field Artillery Battalion (75mm)

Table 4
THE 82nd AIRBORNE DIVISION, 1943

Headquarters, 82nd Airborne Division

Headquarters Company, 82nd Airborne Division

307th Airborne Engineer Battalion	325th Glider Infantry Regiment
80th Airborne Antiaircraft Battalion	504th Parachute Infantry Regiment
307th Airborne Medical Company	505th Parachute Infantry Regiment
407th Airborne Quartermaster Company	
782nd Airborne Ordnance Maintenance Company	**Headquarter, 82nd Airborne Division Artillery**
82nd Airborne Signal Company	319th Glider Field Artillery Battalion(75mm)
82nd Parachute Maintenance Company	320th Glider Field Artillery Battalion(75mm)
82nd Airborne Reconnaissance Platoon	376th Parachute Field Artillery Battalion(75mm)
82nd Airborne Military Police Platoon	456th Parachute Field Artillery Battalion(75mm)

---

setts, and then to New York for deployment to North Africa. Ridgway was concerned that the Division did not have enough time to train together because of all the changes and movements that had been made. He was confident, however, that the soldiers of the 82nd would do their best to make the new type of division a success.

The 82nd arrived at Casablanca, Morocco, on 10 May 1943 and shortly moved to the city of Oujda. The 2nd Battalion, 509th PIR, which had already seen combat in North Africa, was attached to the Division. The 509th made three jumps in November 1942 to destroy enemy communications and supply lines during Operation Torch, the Allied invasion of North Africa. In the heat and dust of Oujda, the troops of the 82nd conducted continuous training to maintain their physical and tactical sharpness. Reviews were conducted by General Bradley and General Patton who insisted that the paratroopers be used to spearhead the assault on Sicily. A practice jump and a review were also conducted for General Eisenhower and General Clark. In late June, the 82nd moved to Kairoun, Tunisia, to stage Operation Husky, the invasion of Sicily.

Because of aircraft shortages, the entire Division could not be employed. Gavin's 505th PIR was chosen to spearhead the invasion along with the 3rd Battalion, 504th PIR (3/504th); the 456th PFAB; B Company, 307th Engineers; and other support elements. On the night of 9 July 1943, the paratroopers boarded C-47s and took-off for Gela, Sicily. The mission of the paratroopers was to land near Gela and secure the high ground. They were also to disrupt enemy communications and prevent reinforcements from reaching the beach. Further, the 505th would be ready to assist the 1st Division in capturing the airfield at Ponte Olivo. The 504th, minus the 3rd Battalion, would be prepared to jump on the evening of the 10th. The remainder of the Division would follow in glider and airplane as soon as possible.

About an hour before take off, each paratrooper in the invasion force was given a small slip of paper with the following message:

Tonight you embark upon a combat mission for which our people and the free world have been waiting for two years. You will spearhead the landing of an American force upon the island of Sicily. Every preparation has been made to eliminate the element of chance. You have been given the means to do the job and you are backed by the largest assemblage of air power in the world's history.

The eyes of the world are upon you. The hopes and prayers of every American go with you.

Since it is our first fight at night you must use the countersign and avoid firing on each other. The bayonet is the night fighter's best weapon. Conserve your water and ammunition.

The term American Parachutist has become synonymous with courage of high order. Let us carry the fight to the enemy and make the American Parachutist feared and respected through all his ranks. Attack violently. Destroy him wherever found.

Good landing, good fight, and good luck.

(signed) James Gavin, Colonel, Commanding.

As the planes of the first lift approached Sicily, they encountered gale force winds which scattered the formations. Inexperienced pilots flying a difficult route at night added to the disorganization. Most of the planes missed their planned drop zones and the paratroopers were scattered for miles. Many of the troopers, however, were able to gather in small groups and carry out their missions. Typical of the ferocity of the American paratrooper was that displayed by PFC Michael Scambelluri of C Company, 505th. Mike landed in an area of heavy fighting and single handedly attacked a fortified enemy position. He was soon captured by Italian troops. When questioned in Italian, he responded in the same language. His captors believed him to be a spy and he was shot several times. The departing troops threw two hand grenades at him to finish the job. Mike walked and crawled, bleeding the whole way, to a farmhouse where local civilians guided him to American lines. After that incident, he was called "Iron Mike" by his comrades. The German commanders were so confused by the scattered drop and many small actions that they thought several divisions had parachuted onto Sicily. Reserve forces were delayed in arriving at the beachhead, which gave the Allies valuable time.

On the night of 11 July 1943, one of the worst tragedies of the war occurred. The U.S. invasion fleet off the coast of Sicily was on alert because it had been attacked by enemy aircraft. As the 504th passed over the fleet, someone opened fire, mistaking the U.S. troop carriers for enemy aircraft. Although Ridgway was assured that passage of his troops was coordinated with the fleet, twenty-three airplanes were shot down by friendly fire. Most of the troops were able to bail out, but 132 were wounded and eighty-one were killed, including Brigadier General Keerans, the Assistant Division Commander. Because of the confusion, the 504th was also widely scattered.

Southeast of Niscemi, the 3/504th made contact with and defeated the elements of the German Herman Göring Division. The 3/505th and a group of engineers, led by Gavin, seized and held the important high ground of Biazza Ridge. Elements of the Herman Göring Division attacked, but the paratroopers were able to hold with the help of 75mm howitzers from the 456th PFAB. The 82nd defended the ridge until elements of the 45th Division arrived with tank support. Using their additional fire power, Gavin's troopers launched an attack that drove the enemy completely from the ridge.

On 18 July 1943, the Division moved west as part of Patton's Provisional Corps to clear western Sicily. Agrigento, Licata, St. Marguerita, and Castelvetrano all fell to the 82nd. By the 23rd, the 505th reached Trapani and the 504th reached Castellamare in western Sicily. The Division received minor casualties and took over 23,000 prisoners. In five days the 82nd had advanced 150 miles.

Although the initial drops of the Division had been poorly executed, the 82nd was able to contribute to Allied victory in Sicily. General Patton, for example, noted that the airborne operations advanced the progress of the amphibious landings by two days. At the end of the war, General Kurt Student, commander of German Airborne Forces, gave the greatest praise to the 82nd:

"It is my opinion that if it had not been for the allied airborne forces blocking the Herman Göring Armored Division from reaching the beachhead, that Division would have driven the initial seaborne forces back into the sea."

The 82nd conducted occupation duties in western Sicily for two weeks. On 17 August, Messina was captured and the 82nd was released from its duties the following day. On the 19th, the 82nd began movement back to Kairoun, Tunisia, to prepare for its next mission – the invasion of Italy.

Several plans were made and the 82nd prepared to execute them, but each time the plans were canceled. In early September, the Division joined troop carrier squadrons in Sicily to continue training. One plan proposed at this time called for the 82nd to jump on Rome and join the anti-fascist Italian forces. A secret mission was conducted by Brigadier General Maxwell Taylor, Division Artillery Commander, to make contact with Marshall Badoglio of the Italian forces. The meeting disclosed the fact that the anti-fascist forces were not very organized. Badoglio stated, "Operation Giant Two is no longer possible because we lack forces to guarantee airports." Fortunately, the plan was canceled while the 82nd was boarding aircraft. More significantly, however, Maxwell was able to obtain an Italian surrender before the Allied landings at Salerno. With the Rome mission canceled, the 82nd waited for its next mission.

On 9 September 1943, the Allies began Operation Avalanche with an amphibious landing at Salerno. Originally, the 82nd was to conduct an airborne assault to seize the Sorrento Ridge, but this operation was also canceled. The beachhead was soon in danger because of fire coming from the ridge. In order to save the beachhead, General Mark Clark, commanding the U.S. Fifth Army, requested Ridgway to make a drop to reinforce VI Corps. On the evening of 13 September, Tucker's 504th, less the 3rd Battalion, dropped south of the Sele River into the VI Corps area near Paestum. The 509th, which was still attached to the 82nd, jumped into Avellino with a platoon of 307th Engineers to prevent reinforcements from reaching the beach. The following evening the 505th parachuted onto the beachhead also. The drops were well organized and on target, which was mainly due to the use of small detachments that jumped ahead of the main body. The detachments, called pathfinders, made fires and set up lights in the shape of a "T" which the planes used as a guide. The Eureka transmitter and Rebecca receiver were also used. The Eureka/Rebecca was an aircraft guidance system based on radio signals. Pathfinders could jump with the transmitter and guide the main body of aircraft that would have a receiver. On the 15th, the 325th and 3/504th conducted a seaborne landing in the Salerno area to reinforce the left flank of the VI Corps. On the 16th, the 1st and 2nd Battalions, 504th began their attack on the high ground at Altavilla. By the next day they were surrounded and under intense enemy fire. General Dawley, the VI Corps Commander, suggested the 504th withdraw. Colonel Tucker responded, "Retreat, Hell! Send me my other battalion!" With that, the 3/504th was rushed to Altavilla and the 504th held. General Clark stated that the action, "was responsible for saving the Salerno beachhead."

Throughout September the 82nd conducted combat operations in the Salerno/Naples area. The 325th assisted the Rangers in clearing the Sorrentine Peninsula. The 504th secured the Chiunzi Pass and Castellamare. The 505th captured Pompeii and was the first unit to enter Naples. The 505th continued north to the Volturno River where it cleared the area of Germans and became the first unit to cross the river. Gavin was promoted to Brigadier General and became Assistant Division Commander. During October, the 82nd was mainly preoccupied with occupying Naples which provided some rest to many weary troopers.

The 504th was thrown into the line to fill gaps and participated in fierce mountain fighting. The regiment assaulted Mt. Sammucro and adjacent hills in the Venafro sector. After nineteen days of fighting, the 504th returned to Naples for rest and to await further combat operations.

On 18 November the 82nd, less the 504th, sailed for Ireland to prepare for the invasion of France. The 504th and 509th remained in Italy to assist the Fifth Army. Both units were used in the mountains of Italy and became highly proficient in conducting small unit patrolling.

The 504th, meanwhile, continued fighting in the Venafro sector of Italy until being relieved on 27 December. By 22 January the 504th was back in action as part of Fifth Army's assault at Anzio during Operation Shingle. The 504th conducted an amphibious landing at Anzio and took up positions on the right flank of the beachhead along the Mussolini Canal. The 3rd Battalion was committed to fighting in the northern sector where it earned a Presidential Unit Citation for actions in the town of Aprilia. While the 504th was operating along the Mussolini Canal, a German Officer noted in his diary:

> American parachutists – devils in baggy pants – are less than 100 meters from my outpost line. I can't sleep at night; they pop up from nowhere and we never know when or how they strike next. Seems like the black-hearted devils are everywhere.

This seemingly unflattering statement was considered a great compliment by the 504th and they still use the nickname "Devils in Baggy Pants." During the Anzio campaign, the 504th engaged elements of the Herman Goering Division, the 16th SS Panzer Grenadier Division, and the 3rd Panzer Grenadier Division. The 504th was finally withdrawn from Anzio on 25 March 1944 and set sail for England to join the 82nd once again.

The 82nd had arrived in Ireland on 9 December 1943. Brigadier General James Gavin, now Assistant Division Commander, was appointed Airborne Advisor for the

Overlord Operation; the airborne operation was called Neptune. At Ridgway's insistence, the American airborne divisions were augmented by an additional parachute infantry regiment. Because the 504th was still in Italy, the 2nd Airborne Infantry Brigade, commanded by Brigadier General George Howell, was attached to the 82nd. The brigade contained the 507th and 508th Parachute Infantry Regiments. Additionally, a third battalion was to be given to the glider regiments. The Division moved to England in February and on 11 March the 2nd Battalion, 401st Glider Infantry Regiment was attached to the 325th as its third battalion. The 82nd continued training for Neptune.

After several revisions, the airborne operation for the Normandy invasion called for the use of the 82nd and 101st Airborne Divisions and the British 6th Airborne Division. Neptune was to be the largest airborne operation to date and involved assigning complete Divisions specific missions. Thus, for the first time a U.S. airborne division would conduct an airborne operation as one body, instead of in a piecemeal fashion. General Gavin chose the base of the Contentin Peninsula as the area of operations for the American Divisions because the terrain was well suited to many Drop Zones (DZ) and Landing Zones (LZ). The many rivers and canals limited the use of enemy armor which could be a serious threat to lightly equipped airborne forces.

So valued were the airborne troops after their combat in Sicily and Italy that General Bradley insisted on their use in Normandy. He also told Gavin that he would not make the amphibious assault without the Airborne in front. Bradley stated:

> On my own front I wanted the 82nd and 101st Airborne Divisions to drop behind Utah Beach in darkness, before we landed. Nothing could dissuade me from my view that these two superb divisions landing in full strength could be decisive in seizing the limited egresses from Utah Beach and throwing the enemy into general confusion.

The mission of the 82nd involved several key points:

1. Land by parachute and glider astride the Merderet River before and after dawn of D-Day to secure the general area.

2. Capture St. Mere Eglise.
3. Secure crossings of the Merderet.
4. Seize crossings of the Douve River.
5. Protect Northwest flank of VIIth Corps.
6. Be prepared to move west to the Douve.

To accomplish its mission, the 82nd was organized into three Forces: Force "A", commanded by Gavin, would land by parachute; Force "B", commanded by Ridgway, would land by glider; Force "C", commanded by Howell, would land by sea. The seaborne forces contained artillery, armor, and transportation attachments that would be vital for sustained fighting against heavy forces. At the last minute, Ridgway decided to jump with Force "A", believing he would have better control if he landed early.

On the night of 5 June 1944, planes carrying the 82nd took off from airfields scattered across southern England. The main body was preceded thirty minutes by Pathfinders who would place navigational aids as they had at Salerno. At 1:51 in the morning of 6 June, the paratroopers began jumping over Normandy. Most of the drops were scattered, mainly due to cloud cover and enemy anti-aircraft artillery. The 505th was lucky enough to land in the general area of its drop zones. A small group of unfortunate troopers, however, landed in the center of St. Mere Eglise, where they were immediately engaged by German troops. Shortly before, a group from the 506th (101st Abn. Div.) landed in the town because a fire was mistaken for a drop zone marker. When the plane carrying the 505th troops made the same error, the Germans were already alert. About an hour after the parachute drop, gliders began landing, bringing additional supplies and artillery. Later in the day the 325th arrived by glider.

Throughout the following days there were many small unit actions. In one such action, Lieutenant Malcolm D. Brannen of the 3/508th killed General Falley, the commander of the German 91st Division. The 91st was virtually destroyed by the 82nd in later fighting. Scattered units quickly gathered and began to secure their objectives. The 505th won the distinction of liberating the first city of Hitler's Fortress Europe when the unit secured St. Mere Egleise at 0600 hours on D-Day. The units of the 82nd also fought at Neuville-au-Plain, La Fiere Bridge, Chef-du-Pont, and St. Sauver le Vicomte to name only a few battle areas. Some of the fiercest fighting occurred at the

La Fiere bridge where the 325th was ordered to establish a bridgehead across the Mederet River on 9 June. The 1/505th had secured the bridge on D-Day, but was unable to seize the causeway leading west to Cauquigny. From 6 to 9 June, A Company, 1/505th held the bridge against fierce counter attacks supported by armor and artillery. With assistance from the 507th, Division Artillery, and A Company , 746th Tank Battalion, the assault was made by 2/401st. The 82nd gained its crossing of the Merderet River. To the north of La Fiere, the 1/325th attempted to outflank the enemy position by using a ford. The battalion encountered heavy fire and was forced to withdraw. Private First Class Charles DeGlopper of C Company drew heavy automatic weapon fire to cover the withdrawal and was wounded several times before being killed. His action allowed the 1/325th to move to a better defensive position to establish a bridgehead over the Merderet and earned him the Medal of Honor.

The arrival of the seaborne elements of the 82nd on the 9th allowed the Division to strengthen its defenses and expand the airhead. The activities of the 82nd in Normandy are best summarized by the words of General Ridgway in his After Action Report to Eisenhower:

> Landing during darkness, beginning at H-4 hours on D-Day, this division participated in the initial operations of the invasion of Western Europe for 33 continuous days without relief and without replacements. It accomplished every assigned mission on or ahead of the time ordered. No ground gained was ever relinquished and no advance ever halted except on order of Corps or Army. At the conclusion of its operation it went into Army reserve, with fighting spirit as high as the day it entered action.

The 82nd was relieved on 8 July after leading the VII Corps across the Cotentin Peninsula and returned to England on the 11th. The Chief of Staff of the German Seventh Army, which had opposed the 82nd in Normandy, reported to higher headquarters that the airborne troops had contributed significantly to the initial success of the enemy. Back in England the 82nd continued training and improving airborne techniques. In August, General Ridgway left the 82nd to take command of the newly formed XVIII Airborne Corps which would control U.S. airborne forces in Europe; General Gavin took command

of the 82nd. The Division prepared for several missions that were canceled, but the green light came soon enough.

The Allies had planned a large scale operation which they hoped, like so many plans of the past, would end the war by Christmas. The plan involved a coordinated airborne assault, Market, and a thrust of ground troops, Garden, that would race through Holland to the Rhine River. The airborne troops would seize bridges over the Maas, Waal, and Rhine Rivers, allowing the ground forces a rapid advance into the open terrain of northern Germany. From there, the Allies planned to drive into the industrial Ruhr region and bring the war to an end. For the airborne, this would be their largest operation, involving the newly formed First Allied Airborne Army (FAAA). Under its control would be the U.S. XVIII Airborne Corps, IX Troop Carrier Command, and the British I Airborne Corps. The XVIII Corps consisted of the 82nd, the 101st, and the 17th Airborne Divisions. The I Corps contained the 1st and 6th Airborne Divisions, the 52nd Airlanding Division, and the 1st Polish Independent Parachute Brigade. The units chosen for Market were the 82nd, 101st, and 1st Airborne Divisions, and the Polish Brigade.

The three key points of the 82nd's mission for Market were to:

1. Seize the bridges over the Maas and Waal Rivers.
2. Hold the high ground between Nijmegen and Groesbeek.
3. Deny to the enemy roads within Division area.

In order to accomplish the mission the 82nd would land by parachute and glider in the area south of Nijmegen. The 504th was returned to the 82nd and the 507th was relieved.

The drop took place on the afternoon of 17 September 1944 and was the first daylight Allied airborne operation. The Pathfinders jumped in first and marked the drop zones. A majority of drops were on target and assembly was rapid. By evening the initial missions were complete; the Grave bridge and bridges over the Maas-Waal Canal were secure.

The 508th, holding the high ground on the German border to the east of the airhead, received heavy enemy fire. On 19 September, Lieutenant Foley was ordered to secure Hill 75.9 with A Company and a platoon from G Company. The fighting was so intense that the place earned the nickname "Devil's Hill." The 508th was pitted against German paratroopers of the 3rd Fallschirmjäger Division. Enemy counter attacks continued until the 21st, but the 508th held.

On 20 September the 2nd Battalion, 505th and tanks of XXX Corps, which had arrived the previous day, attacked the south end of the Nijmegen road and railroad bridges. Fighting in the city was intense as paratroopers moved house to house. To support the attack of the 505th, Major Julian Cook was ordered to cross the Waal River with his 3rd Battalion, 504th. The 504th, supported by C Company, 307th Engineer Battalion, launched a daylight attack across the river in twenty-six canvas boats to secure the north side of the bridges. Casualties were heavy; only thirteen boats returned to bring the second wave of troops. The 504th and 307th continued fighting until they held the north side of both bridges which were crossed by the evening.

Due to poor weather conditions in England, the 325th sat waiting until the 23rd. On that day, the gliders of the 325th landed in Holland along with paratroopers of the 1st Battalion of the Polish Parachute Brigade. These badly needed reinforcements were put into the line immediately.

The 82nd continued to hold the area around Nijmegen after fifty-six days of combat. The Division was relieved by Canadian troops beginning on 11 November and moved to camps near Rheims where it was joined by the 101st Airborne Division, 17th Airborne Division, 509th Parachute Infantry Battalion, and the 551st Parachute Infantry Battalion. All these units came under XVIII Airborne Corps control and were placed in SHAEF (Supreme Headquarters, Allied Expeditionary Forces) reserve.

The fighting in Holland had been tough and casualties were fairly high. On 21 September, Private John Towle of C Company, 504th PIR single-handedly broke up a German attack of 100 men and two tanks. For his action, Towle received the Medal of Honor.

While at Rheims, the 82nd received replacements and conducted routine training. It was not long before the Division was being called on again for a combat operation. Unknown to the troopers of the 82nd, the German Army had gathered a large force and launched an attack in Belgium. The Germans hoped that the offensive would cut through the Allied lines and reach Antwerp, effectively splitting the Allies in two. On 16 December 1944, lead elements of the German offensive broke through the line in the Ardennes. On the 17th, the 82nd was alerted for movement to the area.

After making plans and gathering trucks, the 82nd moved out and arrived in Werbomont, Belgium, on the evening of the 18th. Werbomont was important to the German offensive because of its road network. After moving west to Werbomont, the Germans could pivot north and head towards Antwerp. On the morning of the 19th, the Division moved east from Werbomont to the Salm River, where it deployed the Regiments in a horseshoe shaped defensive position. The 504th was deployed from Cheneux to Trois Ponts. The 505th was positioned from Trois Ponts to just north of Vielsalm. The 508th was located in the area from Vielsalm to Salmchateau and the high ground to the west. The 325th was deployed at several key positions from Hebronval to Barvaux. At these positions the 82nd first encountered and blunted Von Runstedt's attack. At one point during the fighting, the Division faced the 1st, 2nd, and 9th SS Armored Divisions and the 62nd Volksgrenadier Division. After the enemy attack was halted, the 82nd counter-attacked. The 517th Parachute Infantry Regiment and the 551st Parachute Infantry Battalion were attached along with tank destroyer, artillery, and armor units. In the fierce fighting that followed, First Sergeant Leonard Funk of the 508th earned a Medal of Honor while liberating captured members of his own regiment.

The intense fighting of the Ardennes is best described by Major General James M. Gavin, the Division Commander:

The 82nd Airborne Division, still awaiting reinforcements and much resupply at its base camps in the general area of Rheims, France, moved 150 miles with its first combat elements going into position in less than 24 hours. It fought, stopped, and held against the best Divisions the German leader, Field Marshal Von Runstedt, could pit against it, protecting the North shoulder of the Allied line, preventing the German break-through Liege, Belgium, and providing a safe area through which trapped Allied units could withdraw. This it did despite the fact that its lines at times stretched more than 25,000 yards. Then, turning to the offense, the Division set the pace for other units, forcing the enemy back through his famed Siegfried line.

Men fought, at times, with only rifles, grenades, and knives against German armor. They fought with only light weapons in waist-deep snow, in blizzards, in near zero temperatures and in areas where heavy forestation and the almost total lack of roads presented problems that only men of stout hearts and iron determination could overcome.

The battles of "The Bulge", ranking on a par with the brightest victories in the Division's history, also proved again that planes and material are important but the most important essential of all is a fighting heart, a will-to-win.

The Allies assumed the offensive by January and were driving through Belgium and Luxembourg toward Germany. The 82nd fought in the Huertgen Forest, penetrated the Siegfried Line, and arrived at the Ruhr River by early February 1945. The soldiers of the 82nd knew the war was almost over, but they also knew there were more battles ahead.

March of 1945 found the 82nd at camps near Rheims, France. Training for possible future operations was conducted. There was even talk of a jump on Berlin, but that never materialized. On 2 April, the 82nd moved to the vicinity of Cologne, Germany, to conduct patrols along the west bank of the Rhine River. On the 5th, elements of the Division began crossing the Rhine to conduct patrols on the east bank also. The following evening, A Company, 504th captured the town of Hitdorf. On the 13th, the 505th obtained the surrender of Lulsdorf, Langel, Niederkassel, and Zundorf. From 18 to 25 April, the 82nd conducted occupation duty in Cologne.

On 25 April, the 82nd was alerted for a crossing of the Elbe River at Bleckede. Movement by rail began on the 26th and lead elements arrived on the 29th. At 0100 hours on 30 April 1945, the 505th made the assault to establish the last bridgehead of the war in Europe. Initial assaults were made by the 1st and 2nd Battalions during a snowstorm while using the same flimsy canvas boats used in Holland. Later in the day, the 3rd Battalion arrived and made the crossing in British Buffalo tracked amphibious vehicles. The 504th crossed on 1 May followed by the 325th the next day. On 2 May, at Ludwigslust, General Gavin accepted the surrender of the German 21st Army commanded by General Von Tippelskirch. The 21st Army numbered nearly 150,000 troops and its surrender to a single Division was one of the largest of the war. A very brief written document formalized the surrender:

> I, Lieutenant General von Tippleskirch, Commanding General of the 21st German Army hereby unconditionally surrender the 21st German Army, and all of its attachments, and equipment and appurtenances thereto, to the Commanding General of the 82nd Airborne Division, United States Army.

On 3 May, the Division Reconnaissance Platoon made contact with the Russians east of Ludwigslust at Grabow. For the 82nd Airborne Division, the war was over.

The same day the 21st Army surrendered, something quite unexpected occurred – the 82nd liberated the Woebbelin Concentration Camp. The survivors, who were given medical treatment, food, and cots, told of inhuman treatment that horrified battle-hardened troopers. Those who had died and were buried in mass graves were given individual graves in a public place as a reminder to future generations. Division chaplains conducted a service with Protestant, Catholic, and Jewish prayers being offered.

The war in Europe ended on 8 May 1945. The Division moved to Epinal, France, to receive replacements and conduct training. In August the 82nd was sent to Berlin to represent the U.S. in the Allied occupation forces. An Honor Guard was established, and it was reviewed by General Patton who commented, "In all my years in the Army and of all the Honor Guards I've ever seen, the 82nd Berlin Honor Guard is the best." This was a great honor for the 82nd, and the Division is still known as "America's Guard of Honor."

The end of World War II brought a reduction of U.S. military forces. The postwar Army would not be able to maintain five airborne divisions, and a decision was made to retain one in the Pacific Theater, the 11th, and one in Europe. Early in October 1945, the 82nd received word that it would be deactivated and that a less experienced airborne division would provide an airborne force for the United States. The troopers of the 82nd were greatly dismayed. General Gavin received an anonymous letter which helped improve morale:

> And we know that somewhere there will always be an 82nd Airborne Division. Because it lives in the hearts of men. And somewhere young men will dare

the challenge to 'Stand up and hook up' and know that moment of pride and strength which is its reward.

It was soon discovered that due to its outstanding combat record, the 82nd would remain on active duty. The 82nd was the only airborne division which had been an infantry division in World War I. The 82nd also had more combat jumps and participated in more campaigns than any other U.S. airborne division. The Army decided to retain its most experienced airborne division to meet any future threats. In January 1946, the Division returned to the United States aboard the Queen Mary and participated in the New York Victory Parade on the 12th. On the 19th, the 82nd returned to Fort Bragg, North Carolina, where it continued training to be the U.S. strategic deployment force for the uncertain Cold War years.

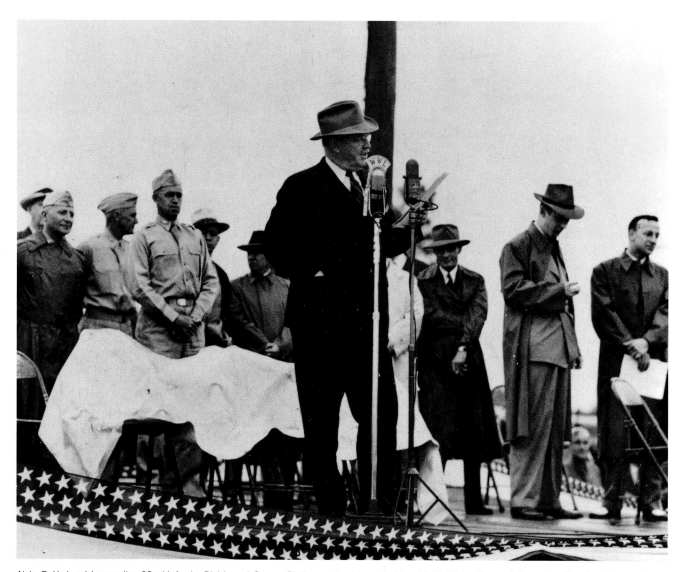

Alvin C. York addresses the 82nd Infantry Division at Camp Claiborne, Louisiana, in May 1942. Major General Omar Bradley, the Division Commander is in the background.

Opposite
Top: 82nd Infantry Division Review at Camp Claiborne, Louisiana, August 1942.

Bottom: Loading an aircraft for a practice jump at Fort Bragg, North Carolina, 1942.

Above: Glider infantrymen of the 325th Glider Infantry Regiment with a 60mm mortar next to a WACO CG-4A glider at Pope Field, North Carolina, January 1943. Inset: Recruiting poster for glider troops. The glidermen did not receive equal recognition with paratroopers until August 1944.

Opposite
Top: Demonstrating the proper door position for exiting the C-47, Fort Bragg, North Carolina, 1943.

Bottom: Urban warfare training at Fort Bragg, North Carolina, 1943.

Major General Matthew B. Ridgway at a railhead on Fort Bragg, North Carolina, watching troops load for departure in April 1943.

Paratroopers from E Company, 505th Parachute Infantry Regiment, practice parachute landings in Oujda, French Morocco, on 5 June 1943 in preparation for the invasion of Sicily. Private John Cages is on the left.

Recovering a parachute after a practice jump with the 505th Parachute Infantry Regiment on 3 June 1943 in Oujda, French Morocco.

Loading machine guns and ammunition cans into A-5 parachute bundles in Oujda, French Morocco, June 1943.

Colonel James M. Gavin briefs paratroopers of the 505th Parachute Infantry Regiment prior to the parachute assault into Sicily on 9 July 1943.

82nd Paratroopers check their equipment prior to boarding a C-47 while the aircraft crew prepares the door for jumping. Kairouan, Tunisia, July 1943.

Preparing to jump into Sicily, 9 July 1943.

A Pillbox in the Sicilian countryside. The 82nd encountered many such defensive positions in Sicily.

Paratroopers inside a C-47 bound for Sicily, 9 July 1943.

Paratroopers of the 82nd passing through Vittoria, Sicily, 10 July 1943.

Paratroopers of the 505th Parachute Infantry Regiment advance on Biazza Ridge, Sicily, 10 July 1943.

Paratroopers of the 504th Parachute Infantry Regiment advance through Sicily, 11 July 1943.

Waiting for orders to go into Salerno. Sicily, September 1943

Paratroopers of the 505th PIR in Salerno, Italy, September 1943

LTG Mark Clark, Fifth Army Commander, addresses troops of the 325th GIR after their operation in Salerno, Italy, 23 September 1943

LTG Mark Clark, Fifth Army Commander, and Major General Matthew B. Ridgway, 82nd Airborne Division Commander, in Naples, Italy, October 1943

Headquarters Company, 2nd Battalion, 505th PIR entering Naples, Italy, 2 October 1943.

Paratroopers of the 504th PIR advancing through the Hills near San Pietro, Italy, December 1943.

The 504th Combat Team comes ashore on the Anzio beachhead near Nettuno, Italy, during Operation SHINGLE on 22 January 1944.

An 81mm mortar team from the 504th in the Anzio beachhead, January 1944.

The 2nd Battalion, 504th PIR crosses the Mussolini Canal in the Anzio beachhead, 26 January 1944.

A paratrooper in England, 1944.

Major General J.L. Collins, VII Corps Commander, with Major General Ridgway, 82nd Commander, inspecting a 57mm antitank gun crew during training in England, 16 May 1944.

Rigging for the Normandy invasion, England, 5 June 1944.

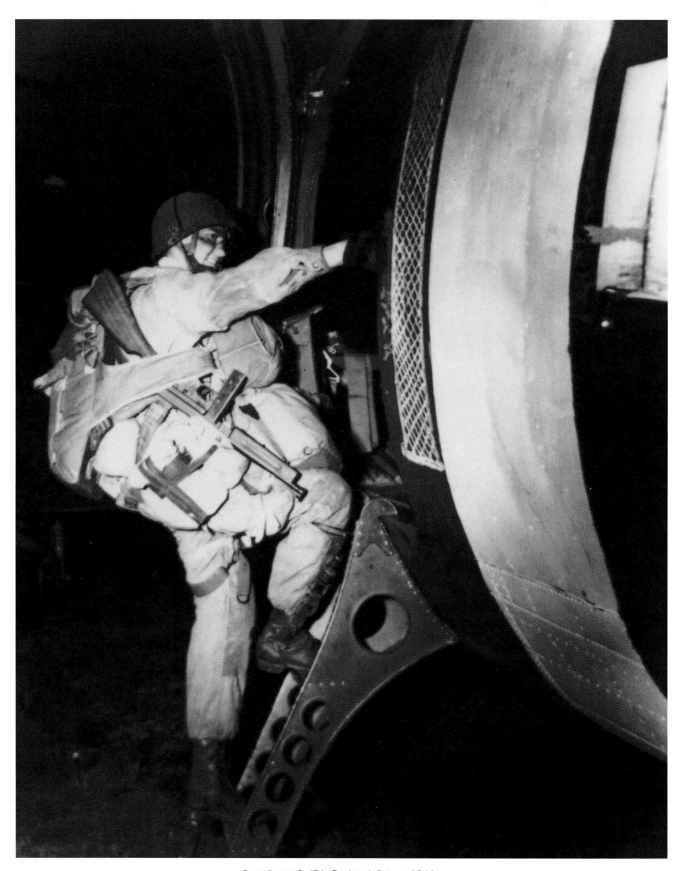

Boarding a C-47 in England, 5 June 1944.

Glider troops disembark from their Horsa in Normandy, France, 6 June 1944.

A WACO CG-4a landing in Normandy, France, June 1944.

Waiting to board Horsa gliders in England, 5 June 1944.

Paratroopers on horseback and motorcycle in Ste. Mere Eglise, Normandy, France, June 1944.

A machinegun crew in the hedgerows of Normandy, June 1944.

A gliderman in the hedgerows of Normandy, June 1944.

James Schaffner, left, and Gerald Arnold (right), 325th GIR, in front of Church at Cauquigny, Normandy, France, 9 June 1944.

Colonel Lewis, 325th GIR, looks over a map with an 81mm mortar crew in Normandy, France, June 1944.

Lieutenant Briand Beaudin (left), battalion surgeon of 3/508th PIR, and Lieutenant Paul E. Lehman (right), also of 3/508th PIR, celebrate their liberation on 17 June 1944 in Orglandes, Normandy, France.

Brigadier General James M. Gavin rigging for the jump into Holland, 17 September 1944.

Brigadier General James M. Gavin briefing his staff and commanders in England prior to the invasion of Holland on 17 September 1944.

A 505th PIR command post in Normandy, France, 26 June 1944.

General Dwight D. Eisenhower addresses the 82nd after the campaign in Normandy. England, 8 August 1944.

Checking maps before boarding aircraft for the airborne invasion of
Holland, 17 September 1944.

Boarding C-47s for the flight to Holland, 17 September 1944.

Opposite
Top: Paratroopers enroute to Holland, 17 September 1944.

Bottom: C Company, 307th Engineer Battalion parachuting into DZ "O" north of Grave, Holland, 17 September 1944.

Operation MARKET begins: paratroopers of the 82nd land near Nijmegen, Holland, 17 September 1944.

CG-4A gliders bring in more troops and equipment to Holland, 17 September 1944.

The first objective is taken: the bridge over the Maas River at Grave, Holland, 17 September 1944.

People of Holland greet their liberators, 17 September 1944.

Armored gun jeep of the 82nd Airborne Division Recon Platoon in Holland, 1944.

A 57mm antitank gun of the 80th Airborne Antiaircraft Battalion in Holland, 1944. The battalion also provided antitank capability for the 82nd.

Sign in front of 82nd Airborne Division command post in Holland, September 1944.

The railroad bridge at Nijmegen facing north. Note the 20mm flak gun on the left which fired upon the troops crossing the Waal on 20 September 1944.

Troops cross the road bridge over the Waal River at Nijmegen, 20 September 1944.

The „All American" PARAGLIDE

NIJMEGEN, NETHERLANDS
TUESDAY, OCT. 17 1944

AMERIKA — HOLLAND

SOUVENIR - BROCHURE NEDERLAND

PRINTED BY: DE GELDERLANDER-PRESS, NIJMEGEN - HOLLAND

INVADES HOLLAND!

17 SEPTEMBER

By Vernon L. Havener.

With „All-American" Airborne Division in Holland. Paratroopers and glidermen of the 82nd Airborne Division — battle-seasoned veterans of Sicily, Italy and Normandy — dropped out of the peaceful Sunday afternoon skies over Holland September 17 to liberate the key Nijmegen sector and pave the way for the sweep of powerful British units northward from Belgium through Holland to the threshold of Germany itself.

The landings — intricately co-ordinated with those of other American, British and Polish units — were a part of the greatest airborne operation in history, and were on an incomparably larger scale than any other all-daylight airborne invasion ever attempted.

Wave upon wave of 82nd Division sky troops from English airfields passed over the North Sea and the flooded lowlands of western Holland and dropped on the Nijmegen sector.

Brigadier General James M. Gavin, commander of the 82nd, was the first to jump in his serial.

The 82nd troops quickly swept aside German ground opposition, had accomplished a substantial portion of their mission and entered the outskirts of Nijmegen by dusk.

Landing of the airborne troops was the signal for the uprising of Dutch partisan forces—including an organised underground army 400 strong. The partisans were credited by General Gavin with giving „extremely valuable" assistance to the Allies. They played a vital role in preventing the Germans from blowing the Nijmegen bridges and gave the Allies much valuable information.

The paratroopers fought for nearly 48 hours without contact with ground forces against hastily-committed German troops who put up a stiff fight as the campaign progressed. The Americans linked

with leading elements of the advancing British Second Army on D Plus Two.

Additional glider landings in force were made on D Plus Six, when the 325th Glider Infantry, which had been held up by bad weather, landed with re-enforcing troops, anti-tank guns, jeeps, medical and other supplies.

Supplies for the airborne troops were dropped by parachute, and flown in by transports and bombers until contact was made with British forces.

Despite growing enemy aggressiveness after the initial landings, the division accomplished its mission completely. With supporting British armor, the division seized and held the vital highway and railway bridges over the Waal River (a continuation of the Rhine) in Nijmegen, thus holding open a communications corridor to the north and enabling British units to relieve beleaguered British airborne troops who dropped in the Arnhem area.

The division took strategic commanding ground south of Nijmegen and played an important part in the final freeing of the city after fierce fighting in the river area. The division took the Grave bridge over the Maas River and two bridges over the Maas-Waal Canal south and southwest of Nijmegen and freed several villages.

Elements of the division penetrated into and held a portion of Germany northwest of Wyler.

Despite several severe German counter-attacks on narrow fronts, the division never relinquished any ground which it covered in force. It inflicted severe casualties on the Nazis and took many (2889 as of 5 October) prisoners.

Orange Above

Dutch Patriots give brochure to „All American" Liberators. This paper is made available to troops of the 82nd „All American" Airborne Division and their families through the generosity of the citizens in Nijmegen, Netherlands. As far as we know it's the only paper of its kind in Holland. We express our gratitude and thanks to the Dutch people whose assistance in this campaign has been immeasurable.

-The 82nd Div.

The famous Nijmegen Bridge, one of the main objectives of the Dutch Invasion (Photo, 1936).

82ND CAPTURES VITAL NIJMEGEN BRIDGE IN HISTORIC 3 DAY BATTLE

504 MAKES HISTORIC RIVER CROSSING

By David H. Whittier.

The 504th Parachute Infantry dropped near Grave early on the afternoon of September 17 after encountering only light flak during its flight over enemy-occupied territory.

The paratroopers, battle-wise from an airborne invasion of Sicily and hard ground fighting near Anzio in Italy, organized speedily, and had accomplished almost their entire mission before dusk of the first day.

Principal objective of the unit was the Grave road bridge over the Maas River, which was taken after a sharp fire fight lasting several hours.

The parachute regiment also captured a stategically-important bridge over the Maas-Waal Canal and seized commanding ground overlooking another Maas-Waal bridge which the Germans had destroyed.

Like other airborne elements, the 504th was resupplied by air during the early phases of the campaign. The unit made contact with the advance elements of strong British forces on September 19.

With the 307th Engineers, the 504th played a vital role in seizing and holding the railway and highway bridges over the Waal River in Nijmegen.

Under the supporting muzzles of British tanks, the 504th crossed the river downstream from the railroad bridge under heavy fire and knocked out stubborn German defenses on the north bank and on the bridges. The engineers, carrying on heroically in the face of withering fire, moved wave after wave of paratroopers across the river in canvas assault boats.

Once across the river, the troopers flanked the Nijmegen bridges and assaulted and took medieval Fort Lent. Three hours later, members of the 504th were fighting 1000 yards north of the river. Hundreds of prisoners had been taken and hundreds more Germans had been killed. Two hundred and sixty-seven German dead were counted on the railway bridge alone. Capture of the bridges permitted British units to pass northward to relieve hard-pressed British airborne forces near Arnhem.

Since these assaults, the 504th has held a wide front against frequent vigorous German counter-attacks and conducted numerous strong combat-reconnaissance patrols.

505 CRACKS THROUGH NIJMEGEN TO REACH NEAR SIDE

By Robert M. Piper.

On 17 September 1944, the 505th Parachute Infantry jumped in the initial attacking force into German occupied Holland. The unit then stormed the town of Groesbeek and aided in seizing the important crossings of the Maas-Waal Canal. Upon completion of their initial missions two battalions of the Regiment organized the south-eastern defense of the Airborne Sector, which was some 11,000 yards in length.

The reserve battalion of this Regiment moved North with British Armored forces toward the important Nijmegen Bridge, focal point of all roads leading north into Germany. This battalion, the only infantry unit with this armored column, smashed its way into the city of Nijmegen in bitter house to house and hand to hand combat. It drove a numerically superior German force out of pillboxes, fox-holes and prepared trenches. They sought out snipers in houses and soldiers hiding in cellars, clearing the town as they moved on despite the fact they were constantly under heavy artillery fire. This force seized and held the south end of the railroad bridge and the all-important Nijmegen road bridge.

German armor and infantry forces attempting to break through the southern defenses, launched fierce attacks at both Reithorst and Mook, Holland. In bitter hand-to-hand fighting, and with bullets, and cold steel, these combat-seasoned men drove the enemy force back, capturing many and leaving the town strewn with burned vehicles and dead Germans. A captured German parachute officer said, „That is the worst hell I've ever been in." On other parts of this broad front the enemy attempted to seek out front lines in search of a weak sector through which he could attack. He shelled the defenses day and night, attempting to discourage and weaken our forces, but the defenses were held intact, screening the Allied move north.

The Regiment was relieved in the Groesbeek area on the 24th of September, 1944, and moved to Nijmegen. Here they assumed the responsibility of protecting both bridges over the Waal river and protecting the north bank bridgehead. Although under constant shelling and repeated enemy air attacks, the enemy was unable to regain the vital crossing.

Division Artillery makes history in Holland on D-Day

The 82d A/B "All-American" Division Artillery made airborne history on September 17-18, when the gunners dropped by parachute and landed by glider near Nijmegen, Holland, on D and D plus 1-Day, successfully getting 41 of their 48 howitzers into action. Leading the way, the 376th Parachute F.A. Battalion dropped howitzers on the tail of the parachute infantry, having its first piece assembled and ready to fire in twenty minutes after the green light. Eight howitzers were in position and firing four hours after the drop, and the other four having been lost during the flight or damaged in the drop. The battalion supported the attack on Groesbeek on D-Day, and covered the glider landing fields on D plus one, one battery being moved by hand 1000 yards and another over two miles to accomplish their missions. Elements of the Division Artillery Headquarters, the 319th Glider F.A. Battalion, the 320th Glider F.A. Battalion, and the 456th Parachute F.A. Battalion, under the direction of Colonel Francis A. March, Division Artillery Commander, also came in by parachute and glider on D-Day, the remainder landing by glider on D plus 1. By the afternoon of D plus one, the forty-one howitzers had been recovered and were in position supporting the infantry. It was several days before loads, landed in German territory and pinned down by hostile fire, could fight their way to our lines, but fight they did, to join their batteries and assist in pumping thousands of high explosive shells back at the surprised Germans.

With the division entirely surrounded by German troops, the 376th Parachute Battalion set up a perimeter front of 360 degrees, which was strengthened on D plus 1 by the arrival of the 319th, 320th and 456th. Moving from position to position, as the infantry moved to capture bridges, towns, and controlling heights, continuous artillery support was provided for every mission. With little or no sleep during the first 72 hours of action, the gunners brought in ammunition from parachute containers, and gliders, only to fire it as fast as possible as the Germans attacked our front. Due to their tireless efforts and alertness several counter attacks were stopped before they reached the outpost lines. The veterans of Sicily, Maiori, Volturno, Anzio, and Normandy, accustomed to arriving in battle with only the clothing on their back, and the necessity of hauling howitzers and ammunition into position by hand, only worked harder, as they fulfilled a long awaited desire to see their shells leave for Germany. It was only with the arrival of the British armor and artillery from the South that they permitted themselves to rest.

As is usual with artillery, observation and communications were a problem. However, heroic action by forward observers, radio operators, telephone operators and linemen kept our communications in almost continual operation. In many cases, forward observers with their parties were actually surrounded in their positions, but continued to adjust the artillery fire on the Germans. Wires

Continued pag. 4

Holland issue of the PARAGLIDE – the 82nd Airborne Division newspaper.

The Poles parachute onto DZ "O" north of Grave, Holland, 23 September 1944. The gliders are from the 325th GIR.

Recognition for an outstanding performance: Colonel Reuben Tucker, 504th PIR; Major Julian Cook, 3/504th PIR; and Captain Wesley Harris, C Company, 307th Engineer Battalion, receive the Distinguished Service Cross from General Brereton, First Allied Airborne Army, for their part in the Waal River crossing of 20 September 1944. Belgium, 20 January 1945.

Below: A paratrooper from the 504th PIR goes out on a one-man sortie during the Ardennes Campaign in Belgium, 24 December 1944.

Major General James M. Gavin visiting the 508th PIR near Erria, Belgium, after a battle with the 9th SS Panzer Division, December 1944.

A 57mm antitank gun of the 80th Battalion in Action during the Ardennes Campaign in Belgium, December 1944.

A German 88mm antitank gun captured by the 82nd in the Ardennes, Belgium, December 1944.

A paratrooper in the snow of the Ardennes Forest of Belgium, December 1944.

Moving out for a patrol in the Ardennes Forest, Belgium, December 1944.

Paratroopers in a defensive position in the snow of the Ardennes Forest, Belgium, December 1944.

Chaplain Joseph P. Kenny, 508th PIR, celebrates mass on 6 January 1945 for men of the 3rd Battalion before they begin an offensive.

SSGT Marible and Pfc Jenkins, 325th GIR, man a .30 cal. Machinegun in Ordimont, Belgium, 6 January 1945.

PFC Vernon Haught, 325th GIR, coming off guard duty in Ordimont, Belgium, 6 January 1945.

Paratroopers from the 1st Battalion, 505th PIR, go out on patrol near Goronne, Belgium, 8 January 1945.

A German King Tiger tank knocked out in fighting with the 505th PIR in Goronne, Belgium, 8 January 1945.

An armored jeep of the 82nd Recon Platoon in Belgium.

An M-24 Chaffee light tank of the 740th Tank Battalion in Nonceveux, Belgium, 19 January 1945. The 740th provided tank support for the 82nd in the Ardennes and the drive to the Siegfried Line.

Major General Matthew B. Ridgway and Major General James M. Gavin, confer on 20 January 1945 in Remouchamps, Belgium, in preparation for the drive into Germany.

First Sergeant Leonard Funk, Medal of Honor recipient, C Company, 508th PIR, Holzheim, Belgium, 29 January 1945.

An M-29 Weasel evacuates wounded near Herresbach, Belgium, 29 January 1945.

Antitank obstacles along the Siegfried Line, Germany, 31 January 1945.

The 2nd Battalion, 325th GIR passes through Schmidt, Germany, 17 February 1945.

Members of the 307th Airborne Engineer Battalion defuse an anti-shipping mine placed along a road by retreating German soldiers, Germany, May 1945.

First Sergeant Lemkowitz, Headquarters Company, 505th PIR, raises an American Flag on a castle near Cologne, Germany, 12 April 1945.

Below: Assault crossing of the Elbe River: Paratroopers from 3/505th PIR on a British LVT-4 Buffalo near Bleckede, Germany, 30 April 1945.

American and Russian soldiers atop a Soviet T-34/85 tank in Ludwigslust, Germany, May 1945.

Members of the 307th Airborne Engineer Battalion with a Russian soldier in Ludwislust, Germany, May 1945.

Lieutenant General von Tippleskirch leaves Mecklenburg Castle after surrendering his 21st Army to the 82nd Airborne Division on 2 May 1945 in Ludwigslust, Germany.

A few of the nearly 150,000 soldiers of the 21st German Army that surrendered to the 82nd on 2 May 1945 at Ludwigslust, Germany.

Mecklenburg Castle in Ludwigslust, Germany: Command Post of the 82nd in May 1945.

Headquarters troops with a Russian medic in Ludwigslust, Germany, May 1945.

Above right: The 82nd liberates Woebbelin Concentration Camp near Ludwislust, Germany, 2 May 1945.

Right: Reburial service for victims of Woebbelin, May 1945.

AIRBORNE

THE "ALL AMERICAN" PARAGLIDE

* EUROPEAN FINAL * VE DAY MAY 1945 * 82ND "ALL AMERICAN" AIRBORNE DIVISION *

82nd AIRBORNE 4 D-DAYS
Sicily July 9.43
Italy Sept 12.43
Normandy June 6.44
Holland Sept 17.44

21ST GERMAN ARMY SURENDERS TO 82ND DIVISION

LT. GEN. VON TIPPELSKIRCH'

Entire German 21st Army Surrenders to All American

By Vernon C. Havener

Paratroopers and glidermen of Major General James M. Gavin's gallant 82nd Airborne Division, who opened the Allied assault on Hitler's „Festung Europa" with a daring airborne invasion of Sicily in the summer of 1943, fittingly delivered a final coup to the crumbling Third Reich with the capture, May 3, of an entire German army.

With his units badly battered and hopelessly caught between overpowering Russian forces on the east and American, British and Canadian ones on the west, Lieutenant General von Tippelskirch surrendered his 21st Army to the 82nd at Ludwigslust.

General Gavin called the surrender of an entire army to a single division, „without precedent in American military history".

The surrender followed the 82nd's assault across the Elbe River at Bleckede early on the morning of April 30. The crossing was made by boat under what Major M. B. Ridgway, XVIIIth Airborne Corps commander, termed „the heaviest artillery barrage since Normandy". Once across the river, the paratroopers and glidermen rapidly stormed over heavily-mined roads and fields, sweeping all opposition before them and capturing prisoners by the hundreds.

By May 3, prisoners were pouring into the division cages so fast it was impossible to keep an exact tally. Intelligence officers estimated that 150,000 prisoners passed through the division area. On May 7, the day the German capitulation was signed in Rheims, there were 34,281 prisoners on hand. More than 2,000 units were represented in the cages.

In addition to General von Tippelskirch and his entire staff, the 82nd captured nine other general officiers and a great deal of lesser „brass".

Vast amounts of enemy equipment were captured or destroyed. A survey of equipment in the division area revealed 2008 trucks and cars, 109 halftracks, 17 tanks, 197 miscellaneous vehicles, including tractors, motorcycles and busses, 89 trailers, and seven eight-inch howitzers. No attempt was made to tally small arms and light equipment.

For more than 36 hours after General von Tippelskirch's surrender, German soldiers poured through the division lines by the thousands. Even in Sicily, where 20,000 prisoners surrendered to the division, the troopers had seen nothing like it. Germans poured in from every direction, swamping prisoner-of-war facilities. They were simply disarmed and herded onto roads leading to the rear. With the Russians at their backs, they needed no prodding.

Roads were jammed almost beyond description. The Germans moved in convoy, not as a military body, but as refugees fleeing the scene of disaster. One could ride along the „front" for miles and not see the end or the beginning of the monstrous queue. A trip of a few miles took hours.

It was the most conglomerate convoy imaginable. With the soldiers were many women and children. Some were refugees; others apparently had lived with the soldiers for a long time.

Many of the procession rode in Wehrmacht trucks, trailers, tracked vehicles and automobiles. Many others rode in wagons, resting on bundles of hay for their horses. The convoy moved on anything with wheels . . . bicycles . . . charcoal-burning and gasoline civilian autos . . . all manner of carts: ox-drawn, hand-drawn, tractor-drawn.

Many walked until they could walk no farther, then flung themselves along the roadside until they recovered enough strength to push on.

The soldiers were much neater in appearance than those the troopers dug out of mountain crags in Italy, or hedgerows in Normandy or forests in Belgium. There was a great range in their ages. Some of them must have borne arms for Kaiser Wilhelm; others had no need of razors.

All night and all day the rattle of wagons, the clop of hoofs, the rumble of vehicles echoed along the German roads.

These were the once-proud men of the Wehrmacht who overran all Western Europe, spilled over into Africa and were at the gates of Stalingrad and Cairo. But, in the first week of May, 1945, theirs was not an army of conquest; it was an army of defeat.

The defeated army was not flanked by rows of shimmering swastikas as it once was. On every side, crude, home-made white flags flew from every house. The army marched over bridges marked for demolition, but never blown. It wound through towns still standing. The Germans did not choose to fight here; their villages were not leveled like so many they had left behind them all over Europe.

The Germans seemed neither elated nor dejected. They had given up the war. They were intent only upon getting away from it.

82ND Airborne Reconnaissance 1st to meet Russians

Grabow, Germany — A meeting between the Russians and the Americans on the Northern Front took place at 9:30 A. M. on May 3rd, one mile East of Grabow, Germany.

Elements of the 82d "All American" Airborne Division Reconnaissance Platoon met a Russian motorized Infantry Column just two days after they had first established their Bleckede Bridgehead over the Northern Elbe River. Sgt. Vernon E. French in the first Armored Recon. Jeep, is given credit for actually spotting the forward Russian elements. Out of a column of dust roared Sherman Tanks with Russian motorized infantry swarming all over them. Roaring to a stop, the Russian infantrymen jumped off their Shermans, and went into a series of wild gesticulations with the waiting Americans. Token exchanges of Russian sausages, Vodka for the ever-popular American cigarettes followed the back-slapping and vigorous hand shaking. Another historic meeting passed into fiesta.

Those in the first 82d Recon. Jeep were: Lt. Joseph V. DeMasi, Lt. Richard O. Prendergast, Sgt. French, P.F.C. Robert S. Bastrow. At 1:00 P. M. the meeting was made official, when Brig. General Francis A. March, 82d Division Arty. General, flew in by Cub and was introduced to General Major (Brig. General) Firsovich, Commander of the Russian 8th Mechanized Corps of the 49th Russian Army. Later in the afternoon Major General James M. Gavin, Commanding General of the 82d Airborne Division called at the Russian General's new C. P. Prior to the meeting, at 9:30 Thursday morning the 82d Div. Recon Platoon had taken nineteen towns in two days, covering twenty five miles since the initial breakthrough on the lower Elbe at Bleckede. Just three days before the Recon Platoon had made the initial boat-crossing reconnaissance for the Division Bridgehead assault.

It is befitting that the 82d „All Americans", so named because they had men from every State in World War I, should be the Division to meet the Russians. The first Airborne Troops overseas, the men of the 82d A/B Division are veterans of ten Beachhead Bridgehead Assaults, geographically ranging from their initial jump in Sicily to their recent crossing of the Elbe.

The Division Recons had led these paratroopers as first ground troops into Naples and first across the Dutch German border. W.F.D.

82ND ELBE BRIDGEHEAD LAST IN EUROPE

First and Last Europeon Bridgeheads Acredited to 82D AIRBORNE "TROOPERS"

Bleckede, Germany — Bridgehead-Beachhead No. 11 for elements of the 82d „All American" Airborne Division was made on April 30 when the 82d crossed the Northern Elbe at Bleckade for the last bridgehead in the European War. It is befitting that the Skyborne Soldiers who made the last bridgehead assault were also in on the initial sock at Festung Fortress Europa two years before when they made the D-Day drop into Sicily July 9, 1943.

Making the initial assault was the 505th Parachute Combat Team which also made the initial jump into Sicily two years earlier. Within 24 hours the assault team had pushed 10,000 yards. The 504th and 325th Combat Teams moved through and with the aid of their old friends from Combat Command B of the 7th Armored pushed 52,000 yards by the second evening. Consolidating the huge arc, the Division busied itself taking German prisoners by the tens of thousands and waited for the oncoming Russians.

With typical Airborne aggressiveness the 82d Airborne, seaborne, footborne mud sloggers had gotten off their French 40 and 8'er railroad freight cars after a restless three day ride to go right into the fight. The night before the assault when Division Reconnaissance Patrols crossed the river neither the engineers who were to man the assault boats nor the regiment which was to make the assault had arrived from Cologne on the 350 mile train ride.

The Russians were met amid scenes of wild jubulation on May 3 and one war for the 82d was unofficially over. Prior to the Bleckede-Elbe operation in Northern Germany the „All Americans" had played a major role in the operation to close the Ruhr Sack. In both operations Major Gen. "Jimmy" Gavin's boys of the 82d were under the 18th Airborne Corps commanded by Major Gen. "Matt" Ridgway, erstwhile 82d commander.

Other beachhead-bridgeheads established or assualted by elements of the 82d include skydrop assualts on Sicily, Salerno, Normandy, and Holland; a sea entry at Anzio, and the vital river crossing assualts at the Volturno, Douve, Merderet, Maas, Waal, Rhine, and Elbe rivers.

During their 371 combat days „Slim Jim's" boys have fought in 6 countries and been assigned or attached to every British, American or Canadian Army except the British 8th which they fought beside throughout Italy. W.F.D.

Field Marshall Sir Barnard Montgomery, 21st Allied Army Group and Maj. Gen. Mathew Bunker Ridgway, 18th Airborne Corps, inspect the 82ND All American Division Elbe River bridgehead. Said Ridgway, "the heaviest Artillery barrage Since Normandy"

82D Swingband Cuts Loose For Displaced Jive Hounds.

While covering the west side of the Ruhr "sack" the "All Americans" had in their care thousands of Russian, Polish, French, Belgian, Dutch, Slavakian and Italian slave laborers liberated when Allied Armies overran Western Germany.

Largest groups were the Russians and Poles, awaiting transportation and conquest of Central Germany so they could be shipped home. Poorly-fed and cruelly treated by their German captors, these people were overjoyed by the meager captured food supplies and limited accomodations which the Allies could provide.

Their reaction to the 82d Swingband, however, was not quite so enthusiastic. Thousands showed up for the show at one of the Displaced Person's Centers but few seemed to understand the music. Each number was followed by loud applause, apparently out of courtesy, but it remained for the "Beer Barrel Polka" and the "Volga Boatman" to stir any visible emotion during the actual playing.

Troppers of the 82ND "All American" Airborne Division captured in Sicily and liberated two years later by the same Division. Ranney, Grisez, Rinkowsky, Manuol and Lindsey.

Other 82ND Division Firsts

In the two years since the 82d piled down the gangplank at Casablanca May 10, 1943, the Division has compiled a record unequaled by any in the Allied Armies. Here are a few of their first and mosts: The First U. S. Airborne Division.(on Aug 15, 1942 the 82d and 101st Airborne Divisions were formed out of the old 82d Inf. Div.)

The First U. S. Airborne Division overseas-April 29, 1943.
The First U. S. Airborne Division to see combat-Sicily, July 9, 1943.
The First ground troops to enter Naples.
The First Allied troops across the Dutch-German border.
The First across the Volturno River in Italy.
The First across the Rhine (Sept. 1944, Nijmegen, Holland).
The First across the Douve and Merderet Rivers in Normandy.
The First to stop, and hurl back Von Rundstedts forces in the Battle of the Bulge.
The first town liberated on the Western front (Ste. Mère Eglise).
The First through the Siegfried Line in the Allied spring offensive.
The First Bridgehead in Europe, Sicily-July 9, 1943.
The last Bridgehead in Europe, Elbe-Bleckede April 30, 1945.
The most Airborne Invasions (4) Sicily, Italy, Normandy, Holland.
More combat days than other Airborne Division, (371).
The First troops to meet the Russians in North Germany (Grabow).

The 82d "All American" Airborne Division has also been in more countries than any division in the European Theater (French Morocco, Algeria, Tunisia, Sicily, Italy, Ireland, England, France, Holland, Belgium, and 3 times into Germany. They have captured nearly 200,000 prisoners in 5 campaigns or approximately 25 per man. Prisoners included Lt Gen. Von Tippelskirch and his 21st German Army, the first army in history to surrender to a lone American division. W.F.D.

A TRIBUTE TO AND FROM OUR LATE GREAT PRESIDENT

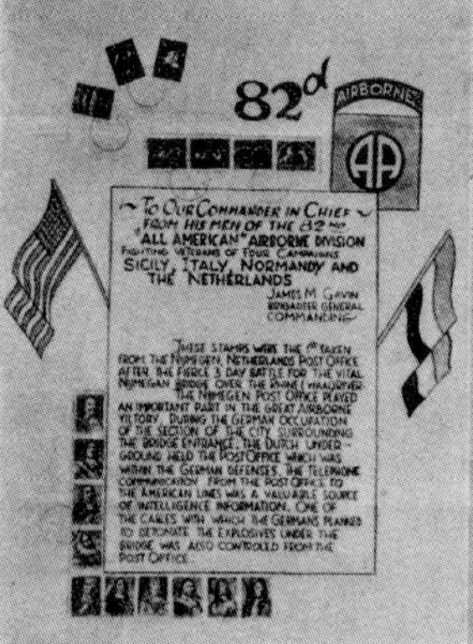

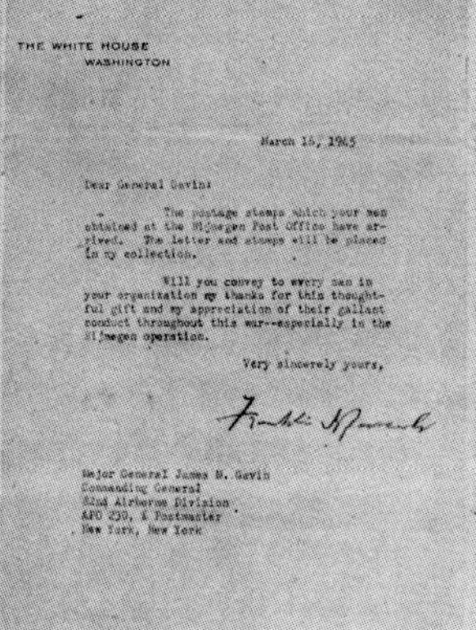

THE WHITE HOUSE
WASHINGTON

March 16, 1945

Dear General Gavin:

The postage stamps which your men obtained at the Nijmegen Post Office have arrived. The letter and stamps will be placed in my collection.

Will you convey to every man in your organization my thanks for this thoughtful gift and my appreciation of their gallant conduct throughout this war--especially in the Nijmegen operation.

Very sincerely yours,

Franklin D. Roosevelt

Major General James M. Gavin
Commanding General
82nd Airborne Division
APO 230, % Postmaster
New York, New York

The Troopers Come Home

500 Kilometer Walk From East Prussia

Veteran paratroopers of the 82d "All American" Airborne Division, captured on Sicily in the first invasion of Europe are liberated by their old buddies from the same division in Northern Germany less than a week before V-E day.

Almost two years ago the first Airborne Division overseas made its jump spearheading the drive on Sicily. Many 82d paratroopers including these men from Combat Bn X, landed in widely scattered groups. Dropped in a hornets nest of Heinies, they fought furiously inflicting casualties on 7 times their number, but by the end of the 2d day, were cut off, and surrounded with ammunition exhausted.

Today, after a 500 kilometer walk from East Prussia, begun on the 27th of January, these 2 year veterans of German Prisoner of War Camps returned to the same division now on the lower Elbe. "The first free Yank we saw," said Pvt Bill Grisez, who looks like Buffalo Bill, "was a Sicilian veteran from the same gang we jumped with. He told us we'd missed the show at Salerno, Volturno, Anzio, Normandy, Holland, the Bulge, the Siegfried Line, and the Elbe, but let me tell you we did some travelling too. Why in Sicily we never even had time to open our K rations. These here are the first K rations we've ever eaten. Say Colonel Gavin is a Major General now. He had our combat team in Sicily. But back to our trip around Europe. First they took us to a transient Prison Camp near Naples. I hear you lucky stiffs took that town later and then occuppied it for a while. Anyhow we were only there 2 weeks and they shipped us by train to Staleg 2 B at Hammersteen near the German Polish border. The trip took 6 nights and 5 days." "Hey Bill, tell them about the maggots at Hammerstein," chimed in John Rinkovsky, Russian speaking American who had jumped the same plane as Grisez and more recently helped talk them through the Russian lines. "Oh yes," Bill said, "They called it barley soup. It was all we got so we ate it anyway, but that barley was full of worms. We were so damned hungry we had to pick the worms out and try to forget it, but it sure wasn't like this chow we're getting now. Some could't stand it, but hell, I'm still healthy.

"From Staleg 2 B they forced us to go to labor farms. Let me tell you about the American Red Cross. Those people saved our lives. Twice the Geneva people came around, and I guess the Germans were afraid to hold out on us, because regular as clockwork, in came the Red Cross boxes. They sent us new uniforms too. Our old ones were in rags. I've hung on to this jump jacket. They got our boots, all but Garcia here, he fought like hell and somehow talked them into letting him keep his. You usually don't talk those people into anything. We were pretty well skin and bones till the Red Cross Packages started coming. I'll take my ,tam' off to them anytime. The Germans always said the chocolate and coffee were American propaganda." "We'd stop 'em cold on that" Lindsey popped in. "We asked them if they could eat any of their propaganda."

"Speaking of propaganda" said Dick Ranney, who joined the unholy four sometime after his capture at Anzio, "we used to sneak a paper from one of the Polish girls who worked on the farm. The news was always 3 weeks late but we got some of the war news. During the Bulge, the Germans said both the Russian and Allied fronts were being smashed. They really believed they would win."

"Yea," said Bill, who seemed to be the spokesman for the group, "they thought they were going to win, but then the Russians started to attack again. That's when we started our 500 kilometer walk. On the night of the 27th of Jan the Russians were only 4 miles away from Dick's farm and 12 from mine. They made us march. We were praying to get caught by the Russians but with 3 guard companies it's hard to stall very much. We started out in knee deep snow with home-made sleds. At the end of the first day they made us throw the sleds awey and carry every thing on our back. It was bitter cold and lots of guys got trench foot, but somehow all of our gang stayed with it, and we've been walking ever since. Two days ago after our guards had thrown down their weapons and run away, we met the Russians. They asked Rinkovsky if we wanted a ride, but do you know not one of us said yes? After 500 kilometers, we weren't going to ride the last few miles.

"There were 400 Americans, 300 Frenchies, 100 Serbs, and 300 Russians in our prisoner march from East Prussia. At least that's how many we started with. We used to tell them the Russians were right behind us. They were scared to death. They honestly believed that the Germans and Americans were going to join and fight the Russians. Those guards had their families, mistresses, and everything with them. It got so bad near the end we had to laugh. A couple of days ago they all took off. They wanted us to take them prisoner but we told 'em we didn't want to cheat our Russian allies out of their prize catch. We got these Lugers when they took off. For 2 years they had us where they wanted us. I wonder where they are now? Nobody even wants them.

"Boy were we ever surprised when we recognized the 1st Yank we saw. I still don't know his name but he had that good old 82d "AA" patch on and I know he jumped with us in Sicily. They tell me there aren't many of those fellows left. That was the fightenest bunch of Joes I ever hope to see. Well anyhow we're back and it's great. Boy were we surprised. We kept hearing of the old 82d all over Europe. I guess you guys have fought in more countries than any of the divisions. We thought sure you'd be home by now. How does this rotation work? We've had a long rest, how about us trading places with a couple of the old gang? They can go home and we've got a couple of personal scores to settle. How does this rotation work?"

Well Bill, that's another long story, but you get some shuteye now and we'll take you down to see your old buddies in the regiment tomorrow W.F.D.

* SICILY * SALERNO * ALTAVILLA * VOLTURNO * ANZIO * NORMANDY * HOLLAND * ARDENNES * RUHR * CENTRAL GERMANY *

The VE Day edition of the 82nd PARAGLIDE, May 1945.

America's Guard of Honor at the Allied Flag raising ceremony in Berlin, Germany, 1945.

The Honor Guard parading through the Brandenburg Gate, Berlin, Germany, 1945.

Major General James M. Gavin with General George S. Patton during a review of the 82nd in Berlin, Germany, August 1945.

Major General James M. Gavin leads the 82nd Airborne Division through the Washington Arch in New York City during the Victory Parade on 12 January 1946.

chapter three

The Postwar and Pentomic Eras

During the early postwar years, the United States adopted a foreign policy of containing the spread of communism. With an increasing global commitment, the Army saw the value of airborne forces. An airborne division could be assembled and deployed to a combat situation on short notice. Such a division also had forced-entry capability – no need for a friendly port or airfield. Moreover, new transports with greater range meant that the airborne was a truly strategic force, being able to deploy anywhere in the world from bases in the United States. The 82nd pioneered many heavy drop techniques to ensure airborne troops would have all their combat equipment at the start of a parachute assault. If necessary, an airborne division could be deployed as a show of force to a troubled area to display U.S. commitment.

During the postwar years, 1946-1957, the 82nd conducted training exercises to maintain a high state of readiness as America's strategic reserve force. Exercises also developed airborne doctrine. Training around the world in varied climates and terrain ensured that the 82nd was prepared for combat anywhere. The Division was also used to test new equipment and tactics. Some notable exercises were Frigid (1946/47, Alaska), Snow Drop (1947-48, Pine Camp, New York), Portex (1950, Puerto Rico), Long Horn (1952, Texas), Snow Storm (1952, Camp Drum, NY), Flash Burn (1954, Fort Bragg), Sage Brush (1955, Louisiana), Arctic Night (1956, Greenland), Rio Selva (1957, Panama) and Carib-Ex (1957, Panama). This small sample of exercises shows the variety of training the 82nd conducted to maintain its preparedness.

There were some minor structural changes made during the postwar period. The 44th, 714th, and 758th Tank Battalions joined the 82nd. These units were non-airborne, but they provided additional firepower and mobility on the ground. The 98th Field Artillery Battalion (155mm) was also added, giving greater range to the Division Artillery. In 1946, the all black 555th Parachute Infantry Battalion was attached to the 82nd. In December 1947, the 555th was inactivated and its personnel were incorporated into the 3rd Battalion, 505 Airborne Infantry Regiment, making the 82nd one of the first Army units to begin integration. Further integration continued the following year with black soldiers being assigned to units throughout the Division.

The 82nd also pioneered tactical battlefield mobility in the post war era. The two leading advocates of airmobility were former 82nd commanders: Generals James M. Gavin and Hamilton H. Howze. Gavin wrote the first manual for training paratroopers and pioneered large airborne operations in World War II. He was also a strong advocate of tactical mobility. He envisioned helicopters armed with antitank missiles, helicopter borne troops, and even air transportable armor. As Chief of Research and Development, Gavin was able to supervise a program to develop missiles for the Army. Howze became the first Chief of Army Aviation in 1956 then went on to command the 82nd Airborne Division and XVIII Airborne Corps. While commanding the Corps, he became head of the Army Tactical Mobility Requirements Board which became known as the Howze Board. The board had the task of examining Army Aviation's role in battlefield mobility. During tests in the summer of 1962, the Howze Board was supported by infantry, engineers, artillery, and aviation from the 82nd Airborne Division.

In 1948 the 82nd was allotted to the Regular Army, ensuring its active status. During 1947/48, the infantry regiments were reorganized and redesignated airborne infantry regiments. This provided greater flexibility for the Division since each regiment could be employed in parachute or airland operations. The postwar airborne division had approximately 17,000 troops. With the adoption of the C-82 Packet and C-119 Flying Boxcar transports and improved air drop techniques, the glider became obsolete and was eliminated in 1953.

Ironically, the high state of readiness of the 82nd kept it from being deployed to Korea. General MacArthur requested the 82nd to support the Inchon landings, but the Joint Chiefs of Staff would not release the Division because it was needed for strategic reserve. With the crises in Berlin in 1948/49 and 1953, the U.S. wanted to keep a force ready for deployment to Europe. Because of the overwhelming number of Chinese troops committed to fighting in the Korean War, General MacArthur urged the use of nuclear weapons on tactical targets. The U.S. realized that it was not prepared to fight in a nuclear environment and began to develop tactical nuclear weapons systems. The Army also started to conduct exercises on simulated nuclear battlefields. The first large exercise involving simulated nuclear weapons was Long Horn, which was conducted at Fort Hood, Texas, in 1952. It was discovered that the regimental structure was not suitable for nuclear warfare. In 1956, the 101st Airborne Division was reactivated with a five battle group structure, and then conducted Exercise Jump Light. The exercise was determined to be successful and the Secretary of Defense approved the Reorganization of the Current Infantry Division (ROCID).

The airborne equivalent of ROCID was called Reorganization of the Airborne Division (ROTAD). In 1957, the 82nd underwent ROTAD and participated in Exercise Smoky at Camp Desert Rock, Nevada. This test was significant because it tested a ROTAD airborne division while employing real tactical nuclear weapons. A composite company containing 170 paratroopers from throughout the Division – Task Force Big Bang – was formed and deployed to Camp Desert Rock on 12 Au-

gust. Training lasted until 5 September. The exercise was designed to answer several questions:

Can a highly trained soldier think clearly and perform the duties of his fighting mission efficiently in the shadow of a nuclear bomb's mushroom cloud? Will his hands tremble? Will he obey promptly the orders of his commanding officer? Will he move quickly?

The Army believes the results will be a helpful guide to its commanders whose war strategy is not geared to nuclear weapons.

Troops occupied trenches only 4,500 yards from ground zero. After the blast, paratroopers cleared a minefield and exploited a breach in "enemy" lines. Exercise SMOKY was considered useful for gaining experience on a nuclear battlefield.

The ROTAD Division was also called the Pentomic Division because it contained five airborne battle groups which were capable of operating on an atomic battlefield, hence the acronym pentomic ("penta" for five and "atomic"). The battle group replaced the regiment as the maneuver element of the Army. The battle group was comprised of a headquarters company, a service company, five rifle companies, and a 4.2" mortar battery. The 82nd Airborne Division contained 11,500 troops during the Pentomic Era (1957-1964). The structure is shown in *Table 5* on page 88.

The Pentomic Airborne Division was designed to be highly mobile and capable of operating in a nuclear environment. To achieve that goal, new technology was employed. The C-130 became the main transport aircraft. Honest John and Little John mobile tactical missiles with nuclear capability augmented Division firepower. The battle group Headquarters contained a platoon of M-56 Scorpion self-propelled 90mm guns. The M-56 provided the battle groups with a powerful anti-tank weapon which was also highly mobile. The mortar batteries contained a 120mm Davy Crockett Section which possessed nuclear capability. New advances in technology were also employed in the signal and aviation units as well. It was during this period that helicopters entered service with the 82nd.

Throughout the Pentomic Era the 82nd was kept in strategic reserve, but was never deployed in combat. In

Table 5
THE 82nd AIRBORNE DIVISION IN THE PENTOMIC ERA
(1957-1964)

Headquarters, 82nd Airborne Division
Command and Control Battalion

Headquarters Company   Administration Company   MP Company   MI Detachment   A Troop, 17th Cavalry

Support Group	**1st Airborne Battle Group**	**Division Artillery**
782nd Maintenance Battalion	325th Infantry	A Battery (Airborne) 319th
407th Supply and Transportation Company	2nd Airborne Battle Group	Field Artillery (105mm)
82nd Quartermaster Supply and	501st Infantry	B Battery (Airborne) 319th
Maintenance Company	2nd Airborne Battle Group	Field Artillery (105mm)
82nd Medical Company	503rd Infantry[1]	C Battery (Airborne) 319th
	1st Airborne Battle Group	Field Artillery (105mm)[4]
307th Engineer Battalion	504th Infantry[2]	D Battery (Airborne) 320th
82nd Signal Battalion	1st Airborne Battle Group	Field Artillery (105mm)
82nd Aviation Company	505th Infantry[3]	E Battery (Airborne) 320th
82nd Aviation Battalion (1962)		Field Artillery (105mm)
		B Battery, 377th Field Artillery
		(Honest John)

Notes
[1] The 2nd ABG 503rd Inf. departed in June 1960 and was replaced by the 2nd ABG 504th Inf.
[2] The 1st ABG 504th Inf. was assigned to the 8th Infantry Division in Germany in December 1958. It was replaced by the 1st ABG 503rd Inf. in January 1959.
[3] The 1st ABG 505th Inf. was assigned to the 8th Infantry Division in Germany in January 1959. It was replaced by the 1st ABG 187th Inf. in February.
[4] C Battery 319th FA was relieved from assigned to the 82nd in 1960 and was replaced by C Battery 320th FA.

1958 the Strategic Army Corps (STRAC) was formed with XVIII Airborne Corps as the headquarters and the 82nd as a key element. Exercises Banyan Tree I (1959, Panama) and Banyan Tree II (1960, Panama) were just two of many exercises that tested the rapid deployment capabilities of STRAC. In 1961 STRAC was renamed ARSTRIKE (Army Strike Command) and was the Army component of the U.S. Strike Command (STRICOM). The Division was put on alert during the Cuban Missile Crisis of 1962, but did not deploy anywhere. The 82nd participated in Exercise Air Assault II in the fall of 1964 to test airmobile concepts. The 82nd remained the key Army division for ARSTRIKE because of its rapid deployment capabilities.

C-82s fly overhead as 82nd troopers march up Constitution Avenue in an Armed Forces Parade, Washington, DC, 7 April 1947.

Paratroopers exit a C-82 Packet over Fort Bragg, NC, ca. 1947.

Exercise SNOW DROP, Pine Camp, NY, November 1947. A paratrooper of the 505th Airborne Battalion Combat Team using an SCR-300 radio on the drop zone.

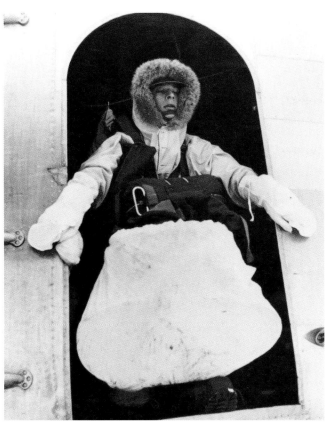

Standing in the door of a C-82 during Exercise SNOW DROP, November 1947-February 1948, Pine Camp, NY.

Paratroopers of the 505th ABCT prepared to test winter warfare equipment at Pine Camp, NY, November 1947-February 1948.

Right: A machinegun team prepares to leave the drop zone with the use of skis at Pine Camp, NY, November 1947-February 1948.

Paratroopers of the 505th ABCT load a C-82 for a jump at Pine Camp, NY, November 1947-February 1948.

Loading a 75mm pack howitzer into a CG-15 glider at Pope AFB, NC, ca. 1948.

Engineers from the 307th Engineer Battalion load a Clarkair CA-1 bulldozer into a C-82 Packet at Pope AFB, NC, ca. 1948.

82nd MPs prepare to exit a C-119 Flying Boxcar over Fort Bragg, NC, 10 August 1953.

Exiting a C-119 Flying Boxcar over Fort Bragg, NC, ca.1952.

An H-19 Chickasaw helicopter delivers 82nd troops to a landing zone during training exercises at Fort Bragg, NC, September 1952.

M-48 tanks of the 44th Tank Battalion in the Division review, Fort Bragg, NC, May 1955.

Practice parachute assault, 1950s.

A jeep being heavy dropped from a C-119, 1950s.

Recovering equipment from a heavy drop, 1950s. Note the jeep upside down.

A jeep of the 82nd Airborne Division Provisional Company unloads from a C-124 at Indian Springs AFB enroute to Camp Desert Rock, Nevada for Exercise SMOKY, August 1957.

A postwar paratrooper, 1940s.

Pathfinders from the 82nd and 101st Airborne Divisions direct helicopters by radio during Exercise SMOKY at Camp Desert Rock, Nevada, August 1957.

Paratroopers from the 2nd Platoon, 82nd Airborne Division Provisional Company, clear a minefield during Exercise SMOKY at Camp Desert Rock, Nevada, August 1957.

A Pentomic paratrooper, 1960s.

President John F. Kennedy visits the 82nd Airborne Division for a readiness exercise demonstration at Fort Bragg, NC, 12 October 1961.

Paratroopers of A Troop, 17th Cavalry, disembark from their H-34 Choctaw helicopter during an airmobile exercise at Fort Bragg, NC, 6 September 1958.

Paratroopers from the 2nd Airborne Battle Group, 501st Infantry, load a C-130 Hercules for the trip home after completing Exercise BANYON TREE in Panama, February 1959.

An H-34 Choctaw helicopter delivers a Little John rocket to a landing zone during a training exercise, 1962-1965.

A machinegun crew of the 1st Airborne Battle Group, 187th Infantry, places fire on their objective during Exercise SUNSHADE IV at Fort Bragg, NC, 14 December 1962.

Lieutenant Strader demonstrates the prone firing position with an M-14 rifle at Fort Bragg, NC, 31 August 1963. He wears the M-1956 combat equipment.

Training with the M-56 Scorpion 90mm self-propelled antitank gun, Fort Bragg, NC, 1960s.

Sergeant Chadwick models the Army's New Look fatigue uniform and M-1956 combat equipment, Fort Bragg, NC, 16 July 1964.

chapter four

ROAD-61: Flexibility for the Future

By the early 1960s the U.S. realized that it could not rely upon nuclear weapons to handle small conflicts. A new structure that employed more powerful conventional weapons was needed. In May 1961 President Kennedy sent a special message to Congress to announce a new structure change in the Army called Reorganization Objective Army Division (ROAD). The ROAD Airborne Division consisted of 13,500 troops initially, but was expanded to 16,000 and finally to 18,000 by the early 1980s. The 82nd Airborne Division, restructured according to ROAD in 1964, can be seen in *Table 6* on page 106.

Between 1964 and 1985, several changes were made in the organization of the Division. The Little John Battery was deleted in 1965. To maintain a nuclear capability the 55th and 56th Infantry Platoons (Davy Crockett) were activated in 1967. The platoons were deactivated in 1968. A target acquisition battery, B/26th Field Artillery, was added in 1977. The 82nd Finance Company and the 21st Chemical Company joined the Division Support Command in 1981. To increase the firepower of the 82nd, the 7th Battalion, 60th Air Defense Artillery, and the 4th Battalion, 68th Armor, were added in 1970 and 1967, respectively. The infantry brigades received additional firepower with the formation of anti-tank companies in 1977 (E/325, E/504, and E/505). The Military Intelligence Company was expanded and redesignated the 313th MI Battalion. The 313th provided electronic warfare support, such as the use of ground sensors, for the Division. With the new ROAD structure the 82nd became even more flexible and more powerful. The nine infantry battalions could be arranged under any of the brigades to tailor a

task force for any mission. As usual, the "All American" continued intensive training to be prepared for any contingency.

The first real test of the ROAD structure came in the mid-1960s. With the assassination of political strongman Rafael Trujillo in 1961, the government of the Dominican Republic became unstable. After a series of elections and coups, a triumvirate emerged which was recognized by the U.S. in 1963. In 1965 the political situation in the Dominican Republic had become unstable again as the triumvirate headed by Reid Cabral was threatened by a coup. The U.S. feared that a civil war might lead to a communist-backed government. On 28 April a small contingent of Marines landed to help protect the U.S. Embassy. With the possibility of losing the Dominican Republic as an ally, U.S. Ambassador W.T. Bennett asked the president to send additional troops to restore order. Stating the safety of Americans and the restoration of stability as his primary objectives, President Johnson ordered the 82nd to deploy to the Dominican Republic.

The 82nd Airborne Division was alerted for deployment to the Dominican Republic on 29 April 1965. Under the name Power Pack, lead elements of the 3rd Brigade, along with the Division Commander, Major General York, landed at San Isidro Airfield the following day. Troops began moving west to secure the Duarte Bridge and the east bank of the Ozoma River. A task force comprised of the 1-508th, C/1-505th, the 307th Engineer Battalion, and the 1/17th Cavalry secured the objectives and sent an element to link up with the Marines in Santo Domingo. By 3 May a corridor was established that ef-

---

Table 6

The 82nd AIRBORNE DIVISION UNDER ROAD
(1964-1986)

Headquarters and Headquarters Company

Division Support Command	1st Brigade	Division Artillery
782nd Maintenance Battalion	1st Battalion (Airborne) 504th Infantry	1st Battalion (Airborne) 319th
407th Supply & Transportation Battalion	2nd Battalion (Airborne) 504th Infantry	Field Artillery (105mm)
307th Medical Battalion	2nd Battalion (Airborne) 508th Infantry	1st Battalion (Airborne) 320th
82nd Administrative Company	**2nd Brigade**	Field Artillery (105mm)
	1st Battalion (Airborne) 325th Infantry	2nd Battalion (Airborne) 321st
307th Engineer Battalion	2nd Battalion (Airborne) 325th Infantry	Field Artillery (105mm)
618th Engineer Company	3rd Battalion (Airborne) 325th Infantry	B Battery (Airborne) 377th
82nd Signal Battalion	**3rd Brigade**	Field Artillery (Little John)[1]
82nd Aviation Battalion	1st Battalion (Airborne) 505th Infantry	
1st Squadron, 17th Cavalry	2nd Battalion (Airborne) 505th Infantry	
82nd Military Police Company	1st Battalion (Airborne) 508th Infantry	
82nd Military Intelligence Company[2]		

Notes
[1] Deleted in 1965
[2] Replaced by 313th Army Security Agency Battalion in 1977. The 313th was redesignated 313th Military Intelligence Battalion in 1979.

---

fectively isolated the rebels in Ciudad Nueva. Relief operations for civilians were begun. Embassy personnel were evacuated on 9 May as sporadic fighting continued. On 15 June serious fighting erupted as rebel forces sent tanks and aircraft against the Division. The 82nd entered and cleared a large portion of Ciudad Nueva in two days of heavy contact. Fighting began to quiet down as negotiations were conducted to restore peace to the city. By late summer most of the Division redeployed. The 1st Brigade remained until 21 September 1966 to help maintain order. The deployment to the Dominican Republic was the first combat operation of the 82nd since World War II. It was also the cause of its first combat casualties since that war – a total of sixty with thirteen killed in action. The rapid deployment and professionalism of the Division during the Dominican crisis established the importance of the 82nd in foreign affairs. Since then, the 82nd has been alerted several times in response to international crises.

While in the Dominican Republic, the paratroopers of the "All American" not only carried out military op-

erations but also conducted many civic action programs. Troopers of the 82nd distributed over 1,500 tons of food, 300,000 gallons of water, and 13,000 pounds of clothing, much of which was supplied by the wives of the Division. The medical personnel treated more than 56,000 people, delivered babies, and administered vaccinations. The engineers rebuilt roads and buildings damaged during the rebellion. Sanitation programs were started and chaplains conducted services in remote areas. Youth centers, playgrounds, and schools were constructed for the children. In the Dominican Republic, the 82nd became an important tool in conducting both military interventions and humanitarian relief.

Even before the 82nd deployed to the Dominican Republic things were heating up in other parts of the world. In 1964, Americans in the Belgian Congo were endangered by civil war. In March 1965, Marines were sent to Da Nang, Republic of Vietnam. In April, A Company, 82nd Aviation Battalion deployed to Vietnam and it was followed by the 173rd Airborne Brigade in May. The 82nd, however, was kept in strategic reserve upon its return from the Dominican Republic. Between 1964 and 1983, however, elements of the 82nd were involved in several deployments.

Throughout the 1960s the Republic of the Congo (Zaire) was torn by civil war. Formerly the Belgian Congo, the nation became independent in 1960 but rival factions and provinces competed for power. United Nations troops were sent to the Congo in 1960 and in 1964. During the 1964 crisis, a platoon of the 82nd was sent to Leopoldville to provide security for U.S. aircraft as part of Join Task Force LEO. They remained there from August 1964 to August 1965. On 10 July 1967, President Johnson sent three C-130 aircraft, maintenance personnel, and a platoon of troops to the Congo. The group was known as Joint Task Force Congo and operated for five months, flying Congolese forces to trouble spots. Again, the platoon of troops was from the 82nd, and they acted primarily as a security force for U.S. personnel and equipment. The operation was known as Bonny Birch. The platoon worked on a rotating basis of a one-month tour and was finally withdrawn on 9 December 1967.

The year 1968 brought the Communist Tet Offensive in Vietnam. When important cities were threatened, the 3rd Brigade was sent to Vietnam. Alerted on 12 February 1968, lead elements deployed the following day. On the 14th, President Johnson made an unexpected visit to Pope Air Force Base, North Carolina, to bid farewell to the main body of the brigade. After his address, the brigade departed to carry on with its mission.

The advance party of the 3rd Brigade arrived at Chu Lai Air Base, Vietnam, on 15 February to make arrangements for the main body. The remainder of the Brigade began arriving the next day. Because many of the troopers had previously served in Vietnam with other units, it did not take long to become acclimated and training began shortly. On 22 February, the 2-505th moved by air to Phu Bai near Hue. The brigade followed by truck convoy on 3 March. Several kilometers south of Hue, the brigade established Camp Rodriguez, named for the first casualty of the unit.

The first mission of the 3rd Brigade was to protect Hue, the ancient capital. The city did not have great military significance, but its fall would have had a tremendous impact on morale of the South Vietnamese Army (ARVN). In conjunction with the 101st Airborne Division, the 3rd Brigade conducted Operation Carentan I in March. This operation marked the first time the 82nd and 101st conducted combat missions together since World War II. Elements of the brigade cleared Highway 1, the only major north-south road on the coast, between Hue and Phu Bai. Most of the operation consisted of small unit patrolling and mine clearing. On 1 April, the 3rd Brigade and the 101st began Carentan II to secure northern access routes to Hue. Units of the North Vietnamese Army (NVA) were engaged and defeated in fighting along the Song Bo River and Highway 1 north of Hue.

The Department of the Army announced on 1 May that it would retain the 3rd Brigade in Vietnam under the control of the U.S. Army, Vietnam (USARV). The unit would also be reorganized as a separate light infantry brigade. Under the new structure, each battalion added one maneuver company. The Reconnaissance, Anti-tank, and 4.2" Mortar Platoons were transferred from Headquarters Company to the newly formed E Company. The Cavalry Troop, B/1/17th, exchanged its jeeps for M-113 Armored Cavalry Assault Vehicles (ACAV) which provided additional firepower and mobility. Other changes included heavier equipment for C Company, 307th Engineers, and the activation of the 82nd Support Battalion to provide logistical support for the Brigade. During the reorganization, the Brigade participated in Operations Mot and Golden Sword in the Hue/Phu Bai area to help protect the Vietnamese capital. See *Table 7* on page 108 for the 3rd Brigade in Vietnam:

In October the Brigade moved to Bien Hoa, near Saigon. The Brigade participated in Operation Toan Thang to stop enemy infiltration into Saigon. In December, Brigadier General Bolling was replaced by Brigadier General Dickenson and the brigade conducted Operation Sheridan-Saber to eliminate the Viet Cong infrastructure in the area. To facilitate the operation, a pacification program was begun. Not only were Viet Cong leaders captured, but many projects were also started to help the local people. Over 13,000 kilos of food and 3,000 kilos of clothing were delivered to local women and children. Ten aid stations, numerous public offices, and several roads were built. Wells were dug, houses repaired, and 100 hectacres were cultivated also. Through individual effort and teamwork, the pacification program of the 3rd Brigade attained local success, though the program as a whole was not very effective.

Table 7
3rd BRIGADE, 82nd AIRBORNE DIVISION
Vietnam (1968-1969)

Headquarters and Headquarters Company, 3rd Brigade

1st Battalion (Airborne) 505th Infantry

2nd Battalion (Airborne) 505th Infantry

1st Battalion (Airborne) 508th Infantry

2nd Battalion (Airborne) 321st Artillery (105mm)

82nd Support Battalion[4]

C Company, 307th Engineer Battalion

B Troop, 1st Squadron, 17th Cavalry

58th Signal Company

78th Infantry Detachment (LRRP)[1]

O Company, 75th Infantry (Abn. Ranger)[2]

37th Infantry Platoon (Scout Dog)[3]

3rd Platoon, 82nd MP Company

82nd Aviation Detachment

82nd Military Intelligence Detachment

518th Military Intelligence Detachment

52nd Chemical Detachment

45th Public Information Detachment

A Detachment, 358th Radio Research Company

405th Radio Research Detachment

Notes
[1] Long Range Reconnaissance Patrol
[2] Replaced LRRP in February 1969
[3] Joined 3rd Brigade in January 1969
[4] Activated 25 May 1968 in Vietnam

In the beginning of 1969, the brigade received two more additions. In January, the 37th Infantry Platoon (Scout Dog) joined the brigade. In February, O Company, 75th Rangers was assigned to the brigade to provide long range reconnaissance. The 3rd Brigade continued operations in the Saigon area throughout the spring and summer. In September, the brigade began its last operation in Vietnam. Yorktown Victor brought the brigade into the infamous Iron Triangle where the unit's mission was to disrupt the enemy's supply lines and logistics base. In October, the brigade moved to Phu Loi for stand down in preparation for redeployment to the United States. For its performance in the Dominican Republic, Detroit, and the Republic of Vietnam, the 3rd Brigade received the title "Golden Brigade." The brigade returned to the United States on 12 December after 22 months of combat. On 13 December, the Brigade was restored to its original organization.

Some members of the 82nd were to see Vietnam once again in 1972. In April, a special anti-armor task force was deployed to counter the NVA Spring Offensive. The force consisted of twenty-four TOW missile systems mounted on jeeps, two maintenance vehicles, and sixty troops. Ten men of the group formed the maintenance contact team for the missile systems. Additionally, six UH-1C helicopters armed with the M-22 anti-tank missile system were deployed. The task force was placed under the control of the 3rd Brigade, 1st Cavalry Division (Airmobile). The first action was against a bunker north of Bien Hoa. The target, which was unaffected by indirect fire, was destroyed by TOWs. The next engagement took place near Kontum where an enemy tank was destroyed. After this brief encounter, the task force returned to the United States toward the end of May. The maintenance team, however, remained until August.

When units of the 82nd were not deployed, they were training for deployment. Between 1969 and 1973, four large exercises were conducted: Focus Retina (Korea, 1969); Freedom Vault (Korea, 1971); Swarmer (Fort Bragg, 1972); and Gobi Strip (Fort Bragg, 1973). In the 1970s the U.S. adopted a policy of Realistic Deterrence which called for the use of general purpose forces. The flexibility and rapid deployment capabilities of the 82nd made the Division ideal for the role and it remained the premier unit of Army Strike Command. The 82nd was alerted for possible deployment during the Arab-Israeli conflict in 1973, the crisis in Zaire in 1978, and for the hostage crisis in Iran in 1979. Because of its intense training, the 82nd was considered the most combat ready division in the U.S. and was selected to be a part of the newly formed Rapid Deployment Joint Task Force (RDJTF or RDF). The RDF was authorized in 1979 in response to the situation in the Middle East. In November, the Division was alerted for the Iranian crisis, but it did not deploy. The RDF was formally organized in March 1980, but inter-service rivalry led to the creation of a more effective organization, the U.S. Central Command (USCENTCOM), in January 1983. The 82nd continued to train to be ready for deployment within eighteen hours to a combat zone anywhere in the world and continued to be the Army's primary rapid deployment unit.

The capabilities of the 82nd were soon put to the test. The island of Grenada achieved independence from Great Britain in 1974 and Eric Gairy became Prime Minister. He ruled by force, but was overthrown by a coup headed by Maurice Bishop and his New Jewel Movement in 1979. Bishop formed a People's Revolutionary Government which was modeled on the Soviet government and it proved to be more brutal than the Gairy regime, employing torture and military force on a regular basis. To maintain such tight control, Bishop employed the People's Revolutionary Armed Forces whose main components were the People's Revolutionary Army and the People's Revolutionary Militia. He also strengthened ties with Cuba and the Soviet Union. Both countries sent weapons and equipment to Grenada. Cuba also supplied military instructors and construction workers to build a large airfield at Point Salines on the southern end of the island and to build military facilities at harbors. In October of 1983, Bernard Coard, the Deputy Prime Minister, led a coup against Bishop and established the Revolutionary Military Council. The situation got worse on 19 October when Bishop's supporters freed him by assaulting the prison where he was held. Bishop and his followers proceeded to Fort Rupert, the PRA headquarters. Coard sent troops to recapture Bishop and the fort. When the troops arrived, they began shooting at the crowd of Bishop followers, who were unarmed. Inside Bishop was heard to say, "Oh God, oh God, they've turned their guns on the masses." Bishop himself was captured and executed along with several other PRG leaders. Martial law was imposed and a curfew established. Sir Paul Scoon, the Governor General of Grenada, and the leaders of the Organization of East Caribbean States (OECS) sent a request to President Reagan for help.

Reagan was concerned with the situation in Grenada for several reasons. First, there were over 600 American medical students on the island. Secondly, reports of large numbers of weapons and Cuban troops meant that the Cubans might be planning to use Grenada as a base for further operations in Central America. Another reason for concern was the request from OECS. No response for the OECS could have meant loss of support for the U.S. in that region. With the conviction of protecting U.S. citizens and restoring order as his public platform, Reagan made the decision to commit large numbers of American troops to combat for the first time since Vietnam.

On the night of 23/24 October 1983, special operations forces were inserted onto the island by parachute, beginning Operation Urgent Fury. On the morning of the 25th, Rangers parachuted onto Point Salines Airfield and Marines conducted assaults on the north of the island. Because of their skill with light equipment, two engineers from the 82nd jumped with the Rangers – SP4 Charles E. Spain and SP4 William R. Richardson of the 618th Engineer Company. The airfield was cleared of obstacles and the 2nd Brigade, 82nd, was able to airland in the afternoon. The 2nd Brigade Task Force was comprised of 2/325th, 3/325th, 2-508th and B/2-505th. Although the 82nd was prepared to jump, Major General Trobaugh, the commander, decided to airland to avoid unnecessary casualties and to have a force intact immediately to help the Rangers clear the area around the airfield. The next day, the 82nd units moved out to clear the island of PRA. Most of the Grenadians greeted the Americans as liberators and thanked them. Some of the PRA and PRM continued fighting for several days. The Cubans also fought, since they had orders from Castro not to surrender. The 82nd also rescued students on the Lance aux Epines peninsula. Although most of them did not think much of the military in the past, they were glad to see U.S. troops. The Division continued operations on the island and captured General Hudson Austin, commander of the Peoples Revolutionary Armed Forces. The Rangers returned to the U.S. and the Marines continued on to Lebanon, their original destination. Control of U.S. forces was transferred to

Major General Trobaugh. OECS troops arrived and trained with the 82nd which continued to look for PRA members and hidden weapons.

The last elements of the 82nd returned to the United States on 12 December. During operations on Grenada, two troopers were killed (CPT Michael Ritz and SSG Gary Epps of B/2-325th) and one later died of wounds (SGT Sean P. Luketina of A Company, 82nd Signal Battalion). There was much controversy about the U.S. intervention. Both the causes and the operations were criticized. The intelligence, planning, and support were not very good and this hampered the action of the troops. However, the outcome was favorable. Losses were light and no U.S. civilians were harmed. Order was restored to the island and military police remained for a year to

ensure democratic elections. The fact that Cuban military plans were spoiled was another benefit of the intervention.

The 82nd was prepared to deploy to Grenada because of its high combat readiness, attained through constant training. Realistic, large-scale exercises, many conducted biannually, have prepared the 82nd for combat and continue to keep the troopers alert. Some of the exercises were Solid Shield, Ocean Venture (both in the Caribbean), Reforger (Germany), Gallant Eagle (California), and Bright Star (Egypt). Additional training was conducted in Panama, Turkey, Wisconsin, New Mexico, Texas, Florida, and many other places which include all types of climate and terrain.

"The gutsiest display I've ever seen", said a news reporter when he saw the 82nd Airborne Division Band leading the troops into Santo Domingo, Dominican Republic, May 1965.

A 106mm recoilless rifle team keeping watch on the Duarte Bridge, Santo Domingo, Dom. Rep., 1965.

An M-60 machinegun position guarding the Duarte Bridge, Santo Domingo, Dom. Rep., 1965.

An M-60 machinegun team in the streets of Santo Domingo, Dom. Rep., 1965.

A firefight in Santo Domingo, Dom. Rep., June 1965.

Two troopers from B Company, 1st Battalion (Airborne) 505th Infantry pose next to a knocked out rebel tank destroyed by a 106mm recoilless rifle on 15 June 1965 during a rebel attack in Santo Domingo, Dom. Rep.

An M-60 position on a roof top in Santo Domingo, Dom. Rep., 1965.

A paratrooper helps a Chaplain clothe a child in the Dominican Republic, 1965.

Right: An M-151 recon gun jeep from 2nd Battalion (Airborne) 504th Infantry prepares to leave Fortress Ozama for a patrol in Santo Domingo, Dom. Rep., January 1966.

Colonel Alexander Bolling, 3rd Brigade Commander, gives a farewell salute as he boards an aircraft bound for Vietnam. Pope AFB, NC, 13 February 1968.

President Lyndon B. Johnson bids farewell to troopers of 3rd Brigade at Pope AFB, NC, 14 February 1968.

Sergeant Leoncio Quiles, Recon Platoon, 2nd Battalion (Airborne) 505th Infantry, fires his M-60 machinegun in Fat City, Vietnam, 22 February 1968.

Captain Tyner of B Company, 1st Battalion (Airborne) 505th Infantry, calls for artillery support during enemy contact in Operation CARENTAN I south of Hue, RVN, March 1968.

Left: Hand grenade training in Vietnam, 1968.

Below: B Company, 1st Battalion (Airborne) 505th Infantry, crossing a field as they begin a patrol during Operation CARENTAN I south of Hue, RVN, March 1968.

Patrolling in a village, RVN, 1968.

3rd Brigade troops call for artillery support after making contact with the enemy in a village in RVN, 1968-69.

An M-101 105mm howitzer of 2nd Battalion (Airborne) 321st Field Artillery, fires in support of 3rd Brigade in RVN, 1968.

Going on patrol, Vietnam, 1968.

PACIFIC PARAGLIDE

Vol. 1, No. 1   Phu Loi, Vietnam   December, 1968

3/82nd Comes of Age; Moves South

AIRBORNE TROOPER TAKES TO WATER—Squad Leader Sgt. Jim Barnes of Saddle River, N.J., encounters unfamiliar terrain in 3rd Brigade's new area of operations.
(US Army Photo by PFC Carl Bach)

CAMP RED BALL (IO)—The 3rd Brigade became a separate, independent unit with its movement from the Hue-Phu Bai area in I Corps to where the Brigade is presently operating, west of Saigon. Brigade headquarters, located at Camp Red Ball on the outskirts of Saigon, serves as the nerve center for the multi-base camp system of the far flung Brigade. North of Red Ball, Phu Loi has been established as the Brigade rear area.

With one infantry battalion and one artillery battery in the area (1/505th and one battery from 2/321st Arty moved south during the end of September and the first week in October) the "All Americans" assumed control of their new area of operations on October 3rd. The remainder of the Brigade was occupied with the business of moving.

The movement of men and materiel, "Operation Golden Sword," got underway September 1st, with the aid of Air Force and Navy personnel. The Air Force, with a seemingly inexhaustible supply of C-130's, flew conex after conex, and soldier after soldier to Bien Hoa, the staging area for the move. The Navy, via Landing Ship Tankers (LST's) transported B Troop, 1/17th Cav and their APC's, as well as the many-faceted Support Bn to their appointed destination.

Constructing a temporary camp for incoming personnel and christening it "Resurrection City," the paratroopers utilized their time at Bien Hoa to repair equipment and

check their records. Not least among the attractions in the staging area was the opportunity to eat in a real mess hall.

B Trp, 1/17th Cav moved to Bien Hoa in mid September. They took time to outfit their "tracks" before moving out into "Rice Paddy Land," west of Saigon.

Headquarters Battery, 2/321st Arty embarked for the staging area the 22nd of September.

Support Bn split their load by sending half its elements by air from the 22nd through the 29th of September; the remainder of the Bn was transported by LST October 2 through 7.

The 1/508th Inf. and a battery from the 2/321st Arty arrived in "Resurrection City" by October 6th.

Brigade Headquarters, 58th Signal, RRD, Engineers, and Aviation were on the way south by the 22nd of September, with the last elements moving out of Camp Rodriguez on the 29th.

Last to move into the new

(Continued on Page 8)

GENERAL BOLLING RECEIVES STAR

CAMP RED BALL (IO)— In ceremonies held recently at Camp Eagle, RVN, BG Alexander R. Bolling Jr., CG, 3rd Bde, received the general officer's star.

General Bolling led his troops in their rapid deployment to Vietnam last February and has commanded the 82nd's 3rd Bde since December, 1966. In contact with NVA Forces in the triple-canopied jungles of the north, BG Bolling and his men were instrumental in lifting the shadow of a threatened attack from the city of Hue. Capturing huge caches of weapons and supplies, destroying communications and killing the enemy,

the men of the 3rd Bde inflicted heavy losses on the 22nd NVA Regiment.

Born at Fort McPherson, Ga., General Bolling graduated from the U.S. Military Academy in 1943. As a young officer in World War II, he led an infantry platoon in combat in the European Theater. He was wounded and captured by elements of the 11th Panzer Division during the Allied Forces' counterattack in the Ardennes. General Bolling escaped from a German prison camp in Hammelberg and was able to make his way back to friendly lines.

He has attended the Com-
(Continued on Page 3)

BG A.R. BOLLING JR.

Search Operation Nets Huge Enemy Cache

During a three-day search mission in an area eight miles west northwest of Saigon, C Company 1/505th Inf., uncovered a significant rocket cache.

Using reliable intelligence sources as a guide, CPT Elton Parrish, Hillsboro, Ore., supervised a reconnaissance team.

"We came across a garden which was half dug up. We thought it peculiar that only half of the garden had been disturbed," said 3rd platoon sergeant William F. Jones, Newark, N.J. "While prob-

ing the soil that was still intact, we discovered that below the surface were several metallic objects."

The day's findings included 34 complete 122mm rockets, three 122mm rocket warheads and one 122mm rocket motor.

The previous day the 1st platoon of C Company, under the direction of 2LT Phillip Hubbard, Las Vegas, Nev., uncovered a smaller cache consisting of one 82mm mortar with bipod, 400 rounds of .30 caliber ammunition,
(Continued on Page 8)

HOW DOES YOUR GARDEN GROW? Charlie's garden yielded 34 122mm rockets and 12 107mm rockets to paratroopers of C Co. 1/505th Inf.
(US Army Photo by SP5 Michael Scholefield)

The PACIFIC PARAGLIDE was the 3rd Brigade newspaper in Vietnam, 1968-1969.

An M-113 ACAV of B Troop, 1/17th Cavalry, RVN, 1968-69.

An M-113 ACAV with a 106mm recoilless rifle from B Troop, 1/17th Cavalry, going on patrol, RVN, 1968-69.

Troopers celebrate upon hearing word that the 3rd Brigade will redeploy to the US, RVN, 1969.

Return of the 3rd Brigade: Brigadier General Dickerson, 3rd Brigade Commander, is greeted by LTG Tolson, XVIII Airborne Corps, and MG Deane, 82nd Airborne Division, at Pope AFB, NC, 12 December 1969.

A cartoon from the 3rd Brigade history showing paratroopers finishing business before going home, RVN, December 1969.

A Tube Launched, Optically Tracked Wire Guided (TOW) antitank missile mounted on an M-274 Mule, Fort Bragg, NC, ca. 1972.

A paratrooper trains with the M-47 Dragon medium antitank weapon at Fort Bragg, NC, 1979. The Dragon entered service in 1973 and was used until 1998 by the 82nd.

SSG Francis Middleton, 3rd Battalion (Airborne) 505th Infantry, secures a drop zone during Exercise BOLD SHOT – BRIM FIRE II on Vieques Island, Puerto Rico, 14 January 1969. The 3-505th was part of the 4th Brigade which was activated to replace the 3rd Brigade while in Vietnam.

Training with the M-29 81mm mortar at Fort Bragg, NC, 1979.

Training with the M-167 Vulcan six barrel 20mm air defense weapon system at Fort Bragg, NC, 1970s.

Point Salines Airfield looking west, Grenada, October 1983.

A paratrooper flies the American flag over Grenada, October 1983.

Paratroopers from 2-505th Infantry in Grenada, November 1983.

Going on patrol in Grenada, 1983.

M-102 105mm howitzers from Division Artillery fire in support of the infantry, Grenada, 1983.

chapter five

The Army of Excellence

The 1980s brought a modification to the ROAD structure as the Army tried to retain divisions with available personnel. The 82nd was reduced from 18,000 to 14,500. The new structure which started as Division-86 developed into the Army of Excellence (AOE). The changes were implemented between 1985 and 1989. The AOE 82nd Airborne Division of 2000 contains units listed in *Table 8* (opposite).

The AOE was designed to make units more mobile and incorporate new equipment. The AOE altered the infantry battalions as shown in *Table 9* (opposite).

The new organization gave the 82nd more firepower than ever before. Today, the Division has more firepower than all five U.S. Airborne Divisions of World War II. Shortly after the new changes were implemented, the 82nd had a chance to test them.

On 17 March 1988, the 1/504th flew to Honduras as part of Golden Pheasant, an exercise designed to ensure regional security. The next day, the 2/504th parachuted into Honduras. Although it was only a training exercise, troops were ready for combat as a warning to Nicaragua. The exercise was primarily intended to show support for Honduras and the Contras, and the troops returned after a short period. Once again, the 82nd demonstrated its combat readiness.

The first combat test of the AOE structure came in 1989 during Operation Just Cause, the invasion of Panama. In 1983, Manuel Noriega was appointed the commander-in-chief of the National Defense Forces which he renamed the Panamanian Defense Forces (PDF). He soon seized power from the elected president. Some-

what embarrassing to President Bush was the fact that the U.S. has supported Noriega. Once he was firmly in control, however, Noriega began to act hostile to the U.S. and attack U.S. military and civilian personnel in Panama. There can be no doubt that Noriega intended to force the U.S. out of Panama. Over 75,000 weapons had been brought into the country – enough to arm the PDF five times over. Cuban special forces, working for the PDF, tried to destroy fuel tanks at Howard Air Force Base, but were stopped. The final straw came on 15 December 1989 when Noriega declared war on the United States. The next day a Marine was killed, a Navy officer beaten, and the officer's wife was threatened with physical harm.

On 17 December 1989, President Bush authorized Operation Just Cause. On the morning of the 20th, the 82nd's Task Force Pacific parachuted onto Torrijos Airport. The Task Force was comprised of the 82nd Assault Command Post, 1/504th, 2/504th, 4/325th, A/3/505th, 3/319th Artillery, and 3/73rd Armor. The M-551 Sheridan Armored Reconnaissance/Airborne Assault Vehicle was dropped by parachute into combat for the first time. From Torrijos, the 82nd conducted airmobile operations against Fort Cimmarron, Tinajitas, and Panama Viejo. The Division moved to Panama City where it took part in the attack on Commandancia (Noriega's headquarters), the pacification of the city, and the surrender of Noriega at the Papal Nunciatura. On the other side of Panama, the 3/504th was attached to the 7th Infantry Division as part of Task Force Atlantic. The 3/504th took part in the capture of Renacer Prison, Gamboa Prison, Coco Solo, Gamboa, the Madden Dam, and Colon. The 1/508th, for-

Table 8
THE 82nd AIRBORNE DIVISION
In the Army of Excellence
(1986-2000)

Headquarters and Headquarters Company

1st Brigade	2nd Brigade	3rd Brigade	Division Artillery
1st Bn, 504th PIR	1st Bn, 325th AIR	1st Bn, 505th PIR	1st Bn, 319th AFAR
2nd Bn, 504th PIR	2nd Bn, 325th AIR	2nd Bn, 505th PIR	2nd Bn, 319th AFAR
3rd Bn, 504th PIR	3rd Bn, 325th AIR[1]	3rd Bn, 505th PIR	3rd Bn, 319th AFAR

Division Support Command	82nd Aviation Brigade	Separate Units
782nd Main Support Bn.	1st Bn, 82nd Avn.	82nd Soldier Support Battalion
82nd Forward Support Bn.	2nd Bn, 82nd Avn.	307th Engineer Bn.
307th Forward Support Bn.	1/17th Cavalry	3/4th ADAR
407th Forward Support Bn.	D Avn. Maint. Co.	313th MI Bn.
		82nd Signal Bn.
		3/73rd Armor[2]
		82nd MP Co.
		21st Chemical Co.

Notes
[1] 4th Bn, 325th AIR from 1986 to 1996.
[2] Inactivated in 1997.

Table 9
AIRBORNE INFANTRY BATTALION

Headquarters

A Company	Headquarters Company	D Company (Anti-armor)
B Company	Scout Platoon	(Contains five platoons equipped w/TOW
C Company	Mortar Platoon (81mm)	missiles, Mk-19 40mm Grenade launcher,
(each has three line platoons,	Support Platoon	and .50 cal. mg.)
mortars, and headquarters)	Communications Platoon	
	Medical Platoon	
	Maintenance Section	

merly a part of the 82nd, was assigned to the 193rd Infantry Brigade in Panama and took part in Just Cause also. The 82nd began redeploying on 6 January and the last elements returned on the 12th. Most of the operations had been conducted with extreme precision. The victory was swift and damage to private property and civilians was kept to a minimum.

Back at Fort Bragg, the 82nd took about three weeks to clean equipment, send troops on leave, and handle other administrative tasks. Then it was back to training as usual. Major General James Johnson, the Division Commander, said of his troops:

> Everybody wants to know 'where's the next mission?' Paratroopers really are looking to serve. They want to show what they can do and serve their country. A very motivated group of guys, and we love them.

It was not long before the question of the paratroopers was answered as things heated up in the Persian Gulf.

On 2 August 1990, Iraqi armor and troops rolled into Kuwait. The small army of Kuwait was quickly defeated, and a reign of terror followed. The invasion had been provoked by long-standing border disputes between the two countries, and by the leader of Iraq, Saddam Hussein, who was trying to gain credibility after a costly eight year war with Iran. Hussein cited territorial claims, unpaid debts, and the liberation of the Kuwaiti people as his reasons for the attack.

The presence of a 500,000 man army on the border, backed by another 500,000, threatened the security of Saudi Arabia and a large portion of the world's oil supply. Freedom of shipping in the Persian Gulf was also at stake. On 7 August, U.S. Air Force combat aircraft were sent to Saudi Arabia and warships were directed to the Gulf. On 8 August, the 82nd Airborne Division deployed to Saudi Arabia in what was to become Operation Desert Shield. For the next four days, the 82nd was the only U.S. ground unit deployed in the region. To face the thousands of Iraqi tanks, the 82nd had about fifty M-551 Sheridans (light armored vehicles), TOW missiles, and AH-64 Apache helicopters. At their positions in northeastern Saudi Arabia, the Division stood ready to meet the threat. It was with the 82nd Airborne Division that President Bush drew his "line in the sand."

The 101st Airborne Division (Air Assault) arrived on 12 August, and other U.S. troops soon followed in what was to be the largest deployment since Vietnam. Army, Marine, Air Force, and Navy personnel with the latest in high-tech weapons all converged on the Gulf. Allied nations such as Britain, France, and Egypt sent troops and equipment also. The 82nd was no longer alone. Allied strength reached almost 500,000, and units began training for the upcoming invasion of Kuwait, which, day by day seemed to become inevitable as Hussein refused to withdraw from that country.

In an address to the nation announcing the deployment of U.S. troops to Saudi Arabia, President Bush stated:

> If history teaches us anything, it is that we must resist aggression or it will destroy our freedoms.
> Along with this call to resist aggression, Bush stated the main principles behind the deployment:
> 1. The unconditional and complete withdrawal of all Iraqi forces from Kuwait.
> 2. The restoration of the legitimate government of Kuwait.
> 3. The security and stability of the Persian Gulf.
> 4. The protection of American lives abroad.

To achieve these goals, Allied operations would be controlled by Central Command (CENTCOM) which was commanded by General Norman Schwarzkopf.

On 16 January 1991, air strikes against Iraqi positions began. For over a month, strategic targets and supply routes were bombed. Iraqi ground troops were also hit. On 24 February, the ground phase of the war, Desert Storm, began. The XVIII Airborne Corps with the 82nd, 101st, and the French 6th Light Armored Division, had been rapidly moved west to Rafha to outflank Iraqi units in what became known as the "Hail Mary" maneuver. The 2nd Brigade had already breached enemy defenses the day before the attack while the 82nd Aviation Brigade destroyed enemy targets. On the second day, the 1/505th, 2/505th, and 3rd Brigade Headquarters conducted an airmobile operation to As Salman while the 1st Brigade and French 6th moved by land. The 82nd then moved by truck to Talil Military Airfield. Iraqi Republican Guard Airborne troops were engaged and defeated. Warehouses full of weapons and equipment were also captured. Within four days the war was over. For the first time since World War II, both the 82nd and 101st were committed in their entirety to combat and conducted large airborne (air assault/air movement) operations together under XVIII Airborne Corps. With their most recent combat mission completed, the All Americans began returning home on 7 March. The 82nd was home by April.

Back at Fort Bragg, the 82nd resumed its training and held its annual review in May 1991. The 82nd also celebrated its 50th Anniversary as an airborne division in August 1992. Although many Army units faced reduction or deactivation, the 82nd was maintained at full combat strength because of its unique capabilities. After returning from the Persian Gulf, the Division was called upon to patrol U.S. borders and assist in Hurricane Andrew relief.

The 2nd Battalion, 504th PIR parachutes into Honduras on 18 March 1988 during Exercise GOLDEN PHEASANT.

82nd Airborne Division paratroopers with a Honduran soldier during Exercise GOLDEN PHEASANT in Honduras, March 1988.

Torrijos International Airport looking north. This was the approach to the drop zone for the 82nd's assault into Panama on 20 December 1989.

Major General James H. Johnson, Jr. leads the 82nd Airborne Division Assault Command Post off Torrijos Airfield after the parachute assault into Panama on 20 December 1989.

The 82nd Airborne Division moves off Torrijos Airfield, Panam, 20 December 1989.

An M-551 Sheridan of C Company, 3/73rd Armor outside the Papal Nunciature in Panama City, Panama, December 1989. Noriega sought sanctuary there on 24 December 1989.

Troops from B Company, 2/505th PIR conducting training in Saudi Arabia, 1990.

MOUT (Military Operations in Urban Terrain) training in Saudi Arabia, 1990.

An M-551 Sheridan of the 3/73rd Armor in Saudi Arabia, 1990. Note the mud camouflage applied by the crew in country.

An LAV-25 of the 3/73rd Armor on convoy escort with2/505th PIR in Saudi Arabia, 1990.

Specialist Sharon of B Company, 2/505th PIR carrying a 60mm mortar in Saudi Arabia, 1990.

Combined arms training: An M-551 Sheridan supports infantry training during an exercise in Saudi Arabia, 1990.

Specialist Paul Fisher, left, and Private First Class John O'Sullivan, right, of Scout Platoon, 2/325th AIR, display an Iraqi flag on the Iraqi-Saudi border at Objective Falcon, 18 February 1991.

An M-102 105 mm from the 319th Field Artillery fires in support of operations in the Gulf War, 1991.

An M-551 Sheridan of B Company, 3/73rd Armor carries troops of 2nd Brigade into Iraq on 23 February 1991.

B Company, 2/505th PIR boarding UH-60 Blackhawk helicopters at Rafha, Saudi Arabia, for an air assault into Iraq, February 1991.

The 3rd Platoon, B Company, 2/505th PIR deploying for combat outside an ammunition storage facility near Suq Ash Shuyukh, Iraq, February 1991.

SGT John Village, B Company, 2/505th PIR, prepares his squad to assault an ammunition storage facility near Suq Ash Shuyukh, Iraq, February 1991.

L to R: SPC Cabrara of C/1/319th FA, SPC Kennis of Scouts 2/505th PIR, and SGT Leavitt of Scouts 2/505th PIR in an Iraqi warehouse.

SGT Mark Lahan, B Company, 2/505th PIR, in an Iraqi munitions warehouse near Suq Ash Shuyukh, February 1991.

Gulf War Campaign Streamers are added to the 82nd Airborne Division colors.

A training parachute assault at Fort Bragg, NC, 1990s.

This posed photo shows command and control during an airborne operation at Fort Bragg, NC, ca. 1990.

The Gulf War victory parade in New York City, 1991.

A paratrooper prepares to land with his T-10C parachute, Fort Bragg, NC, 1990s.

chapter six

Keeping the Peace: Civil Disturbance, Humanitarian, and Peacekeeping Operations

Keeping the peace is nothing new to the 82nd Airborne Division. For over thirty years, the 82nd has participated in civil disturbance, civic action, and peacekeeping operations while also being ready to perform combat operations. Although civil disturbance operations are covered in routine training, peacekeeping and humanitarian operations offer a more unique challenge. Some of the deployments were minor, or only required the Division to be held in reserve. These operations will not be discussed in detail, but will be listed at the end of the chapter.

The year 1967 was a time of turmoil within the United States. A confrontation between police and blacks in Detroit led to major rioting during July. The National Guard was called out, but it soon became apparent that they were not sufficiently trained to handle civil disturbances. The National Guard often responded to sniper fire with heavy weapons, causing additional damage and unnecessary casualties. On 24 July, the 3rd Brigade, 82nd Airborne Division, deployed to Selfridge Air Force Base, about 30 miles from Detroit. The troops were taken by bus to the city where they helped to restore order. The combat experienced troops of the 82nd responded only with sufficient force necessary to stop violence. No casualties were received by the Division. The troops were withdrawn from the city on 30 July and redeployed on 6 August 1967.

The next large civil disturbance deployment for the 82nd was in 1968. In response to riots started because of the assassination of Martin Luther King, Jr., the 1st Brigade, reinforced by elements of the 2nd Brigade (1-325th and 2-325th), was deployed under the name Task Force

82 to Washington, D.C., on 5 April. Arson and looting had begun on the night of the 4th shortly after the announcement of King's death. Task Force 82 formed part of the larger Task Force Washington that was created to restore order. The troops began patrolling on the 6th and remained active until the 12th. The 1st Brigade began returning to Fort Bragg on the evening of the 12th, and the remainder of Task Force 82 returned by the 15th.

With the 3rd Brigade in Vietnam and the 1st Brigade in Washington, only one brigade remainded to handle emergencies. To bring the Division up to strength, the 4th Brigade, 82nd Airborne Division, was activated on 15 July 1968. The 4th Brigade contained the 4-325th, 3-504th, and 3-505th Infantry. The 3-320th Artillery and K Troop, 17th Cavalry were activated to support the Brigade. The 4th Brigade deployed to Washington, D. C., in November of 1969 to help maintain order during the Moratorium parade. The demonstration was the largest, and most peaceful, anti-war demonstration. The 4th Brigade remained active until 15 December 1969 when the 3rd Brigade returned from Vietnam.

In the 1970s a civic action program was conceived to improve strained public relations in the wake of Vietnam. Playgrounds, athletic fields, and schools were constructed in nearby communities. The 307th Engineer Battalion and the 618th Light Equipment Company proved very valuable in these operations. The 307th Medical Battalion also participated by supplying medical personnel to assist in local hospitals. Such civic action programs provided realistic training for the Division while helping the civilian community and improving public relations as well.

The year 1980 found the 82nd once again performing a civil disturbance mission. Approximately 5,000 Cuban refugees from the Mariel boatlift were being processed at Fort Indiantown Gap, Pennsylvania, for resettlement. A group of Cubans began rioting because of delays in the processing. The State Department requested assistance from available troops. A unit from the 82nd, B Company, 1-325th Infantry was conducting training at the base and was alerted on 5 August. The 1-504th, 1-505th, and 1-325th soon followed. The troops assisted the U.S. Border Patrol and the situation was soon under control. Night vision goggles were successfully employed at check points and on patrols. Such devices became increasingly important on the battlefield also. The troops returned from Fort Indiantown Gap on 10 October.

In 1982, a more unusual mission was conceived for the 82nd. After several years of negotiating and some assistance from the United States, Egypt and Israel reached a settlement over the disputed lands in the Sinai. In April, Task Force 1-505 landed in the Sinai to begin peacekeeping duties as the U.S. contingent of the Multi-National Force and Observers (MFO). The force consisted of the 1-505th Infantry, fire support teams of the 1/319th

Artillery, a ground surveillance team of the 313th MI Battalion, C Company 82nd Aviation Battalion, and an element of the 82nd Military Police. The primary sector of responsibility was on the east coast of the Sinai from Elat in the north to Sharm El Sheikh in the south. The island of Tiran was also manned by the task force. From 1982 to 1989 the 82nd and 101st rotated on a six month tour in the Sinai with no incidents. In 1989, other units were added to the MFO duty. The 82nd achieved another first in 1994 when the 4/505th PIR began its tour in the Sinai – it was the first battalion comprised of Active Duty, Reserve, and National Guard troops to conduct peacekeeping with the MFO. Of all the missions the 82nd has ever had to conduct, the MFO duty is one of the most forgotten and yet one of the most successful. In the eighteen years since the MFO has been in existence, there has been peace in a region which had four conflicts in twenty-five years.

A new type of operation for the 82nd was a humanitarian relief effort in the wake of Hurricane Andrew. The storm hit Florida on 24 August 1992 and caused widespread destruction along with over twenty deaths. On the 29th, Task Force All-American began deployment to

---

Table 10
82nd AIRBORNE DIVISION DEPLOYMENTS

As Part of The Multinational Force and Observers (MFO) In The Sinai

1982	16 Mar to 10 Sep:	1st Battalion (Airborne) 505th Infantry was the first to perform MFO duty.
		It helped to create the demarcation zone between Egypt and Israel.
1983	Feb – Aug	2nd Battalion (Airborne) 508 Infantry
1984	Feb – Jul	1st Battalion, 325th Airborne Infantry
1985	Jan – Jul	1st Battalion (Airborne) 508th Infantry
1986	May – Nov	2nd Battalion, 504th Parachute Infantry
1987-1988	Oct – Mar	2nd Battalion, 325th Airborne Infantry
1989-1990	Sep – Mar	2nd Battalion, 505th Parachute Infantry
1993	Jan – Jul	1st Battalion, 504th Parachute Infantry
1994	Jan – Jul	4th Battalion, 325th Airborne Infantry
1995	Jan – Jul	4th Battalion, 505th Parachute Infantry
		(Regular Army, USAR, & ARNG)
1996	Jan – Jul	3rd Battalion, 504th Parachute Infantry
1998	Jan – Jul	1st Battalion, 325th Airborne Infantry
2000-2001	Jul – Jan	2nd Battalion, 505th Parachute Infantry

Table 11
82nd AIRBORNE DIVISION

Civil Disturbance Deployments

1962 (1-10 October): The 82nd Airborne Division was deployed to Columbus AFB, Mississippi, as part of Operation RAPID ROAD. The deployment was in support of school desegregation during the James Meredith case.

1963 (12-13 May): One company of the 1st Airborne Battle Group, 325th Infantry, was deployed to Maxwell AFB, Alabama. Although a limited desegregation plan had been worked out for Birmingham, some radical whites rejected it and bombed the house where Martin Luther King, Jr. was staying. The incident led to rioting which began to subside after two days.

1967 (24 July to 6 August): The 3rd Brigade deployed to Detroit, Michigan, as part of Task Force Detroit. Racial tensions had caused rioting and arson.

1967 (20-23 October): The 1st Brigade, as part of Task Force Washington, deployed to Washington, D.C., in response to anti-war demonstrations. The troops were held in reserve.

1968 (5-15 April): The 1st Brigade and elements of the 2nd Brigade (1st and 2nd Battalions, 325th Infantry) were sent to Washington, D.C., as Task Force 82, a part of Task Force Washington. The deployed was ordered due to violence arising from the assassination of Martin Luther King, Jr.

1969 (18-21 January): the 2nd Battalion along with B and C Companies of the 1st Battalion, (Airborne) 504th Infantry, and personnel from the 82nd Military Police Company, formed an honor cordon for the inauguration of President Nixon on 20 January. Some anti-war protestors began throwing objects, but they were quickly dispersed.

1969 (12-17 November): The 4th Brigade, as part of Task Force Washington, deployed to Washington, D.C., to maintain order during the Moratorium Parade.

1970 (29 April to 4 May): Division Headquarters and the 2nd Brigade deployed to Westover AFB, Massachusetts. The troops were held in reserve for possible use during student ant-war protests in New Haven, Connecticut.

1971 (1-5 May): The 2nd and 3rd Brigades deployed to Washington, D.C., during Operation GARDEN PLOT in response to ant-war demonstrations.

1972 (7-15 July and 18-25 August): Division Headquarters and the 1st Brigade deployed to Miami, Florida, to assist police during the Republican and Democratic National Conventions.

1980 (5 August to 10 October): The 1-325th, 1-504th, and 1-505th were rotated to Fort Indiantown Gap, Pennsylvania. The units assisted federal authorities with the processing of Cuban refugees after a group of approximately 200 began rioting.

1992 (29 August to 28 September): Task Force All American, comprised of 2/325th AIR, 4/235th AIR, 2/504th PIR, 2/319th AFAR, with elements of 3/73rd Armor, 307th Engineer Bn., 82nd Aviation Brigade, 82nd Discom, and 82nd MP Company, deployed to south Florida to prevent looting and provide humanitarian aid.

1994-1995 (December to January): The 2nd Battalion, 505th PIR deployed to Panama during Operation SAFE HAVEN in response to rioting by Cuban refugees.

Florida. The task force was comprised of the 2/325th, 4/325th, 2/504th, 2/319th, and elements from 3/73rd Armor, 307th Engineers, 82nd Aviation Brigade, 82nd Discom, and 82nd MP Company. The 82nd helped to prevent looting and distributed food and other badly needed supplies.

With an increased role for the United States in United Nation's peacekeeping operations, the 82nd has been called upon more frequently to supply small contingents. When the invasion of Haiti was canceled in September of 1994, elements of the 82nd's 3rd Battalion, 73rd Armor were called upon to support peacekeeping in Operation Uphold Democracy. Paratroopers of the 3/73rd served in Haiti from 26 September until 25 October. Additional troops from B Company, 1/325th and A Company, 2/325th performed peacekeeping duty in Haiti under the United

Nations during Operation Tropical Eagle between 26 May and 30 October 1995. Between August and November 1996, elements of 1/504th performed security operations in Haiti to support Exercise Fair Winds. The 2/505th deployed to Panama from December 1994 to January 1995 for Operation Safe Haven in response to riots of Cuban refugees.

With the collapse of communist Yugoslavia and the following civil war, the United States committed troops to a United Nations effort to restore peace. Troops of the 82nd Airborne Division's 49th Public Affairs Detachment and 2/82nd Aviation deployed to Bosnia in support of Operation Joint Guardian I. Further to the south, violence was erupting between ethnic Albanians and Serbians in Kosovo. In April of 1999, 2/505th PIR, with B Company, 3/505th PIR attached, deployed to Albania for Operation Noble Anvil. Their mission was to defend forward area refueling points for attack helicopters in the event of a ground war with Serbia. After a successful air campaign by NATO, the Serbians agreed to withdraw from Kosovo. The 2/505th PIR moved to Macedonia to stage for their movement into Kosovo for Operation Joint Guardian II. On 12 June, A Company air assaulted into Kosovo to es-

tablish a base camp. The rest of the battalion followed to establish Camp Bondsteel as the center of U.S. presence in Kosovo. Once again, paratroopers of the 82nd Airborne Division were prepared for combat, but quickly assumed peacekeeping duties as the situation dictated. The initial mission was to insure the withdrawal of Serbian forces and to protect ethnic Albanian civilians. The Kosovo Liberation Army, composed of ethnic Albanians, however, began retaliating against Serbian civilians. True to their commitment as peacekeepers, the paratroopers began intense patrolling to stop all violence and began confiscating weapons. Additionally, humanitarian operations were conducted; clothing, food, toys, and medical care were provided for the local civilians. On 9 September 1999, the 3/504th PIR departed Fort Bragg to replace the 2/505th PIR in Kosovo. The 3/504th PIR continued peacekeeping and humanitarian operations. The 3/504th PIR also operated with French soldiers and troops from the United Arab Emirates. The 3/504th PIR returned to the U.S. in March 2000.

In January 2001, the 1/325th AIR began a six month tour in Kosovo.

An 82nd MP keeping watch at the entrance to Task Force 82 headquarters in Washington, DC, April 1968.

Paratroopers from the 1st Battalion (Airborne) 508th Infantry in front of their command post in Detroit, Michigan, July 1967.

Paratroopers from the 82nd Military Police Company patrol the streets of Washington, DC, April 1968.

A paratrooper amid the destruction caused by riots in Washington, DC, April 1968.

Keeping watch at the US Capitol, Washington, DC, April 1968.

Keeping order on the mall: A paratrooper of Task Force 82 during civil disturbance operations in Washington, DC April 1968.

First in the Sinai: The 1st Battalion (Airborne) 505th Infantry shortly after arriving in the Sinai for peacekeeping duty in April, 1982.

An MFO observation post in the Sinai, 1995.

SSG Mark Lahan, B Company, 2/505th PIR, during a night patrol in the Sinai, fall 1989. He wears the PVS-7B night vision goggles, six color desert battle dress uniform, and night desert camouflage parka.

Two troopers from 4/505th PIR pose in front of a unit sign in the Sinai, 1995. This was the first US unit in the MFO to contain Active Duty, Reserve, and National Guard soldiers.

Color Guard of the 4/505th PIR in the Sinai, 1995.

Two troopers of 4/505th PIR take a water break during a road march in the Sinai, 1995. Note the orange helmet covers to identify them as MFO troops.

Task Force ANDREW, Florida, 1992: Paratroopers from the 504th PIR distribute bags of ice. Note the soldier in the center is a combat veteran of Panama.

A paratrooper of the 82nd holds a little girl during humanitarian relief efforts in the wake of Hurricane Andrew, Florida, August 1992.

Paratroopers from 2/505th PIR in full riot gear, Panama, December 1994.

A crew from the 3/73rd Armor on their M-551 Sheridan Armored Reconnaissance/ Airborne Assault Vehicle in Port-Au-Prince, Haiti, September 1994.

Left: Keeping watch while Cuban refugees are processed in Panama, December 1994.

Operation SAFE HAVEN: Paratroopers from 2/505th PIR practice civil disturbance formations and tactics in Panama, December 1994.

A paratrooper from 2/505th PIR keeps careful watch with shotgun in hand while Cuban refugees are processed in Panama, December 1994.

Paratroopers of the 325th AIR provide security for President Aristide in Port-Au-Prince, Haiti, 1995.

Going out on patrol: Paratroopers from the 325th AIR during Operation TROPICAL EAGLE in Haiti, 1995. Note blue helmet covers to identify them as UN troops.

Opposite: Prepared for anything! A paratrooper from 2/505th PIR in full riot gear in Panama, December 1994.

Air Assault into Kosovo: The second lift of A company, 2/505th PIR arrives in Kosovo to establish Camp Bond Steel.

Specialist Dunham of A Company, 2/505th PIR, on patrol in Kosovo, summer 1999.

Paratroopers from 2/505th PIR distribute clothing collected by the family support group to children in Kosovo, 1999.

B Company, 3/504th PIR on patrol in Mitrovica, Kosovo, 2000.

B Company, 3/504th PIR prepares for a night patrol in Mitrovica, Kosovo, 2000. Photographed with night vision device.

An M-119 105mmm howitzer from C Battery, 3/319th Airborne Field Artillery, conducting a live fire exercise in Macedonia, 2000.

Appendices

APPENDIX 1

Lineage and Honors for Headquarters and Headquarters Company

82nd Airborne Division (All American)

Constituted 5 August 1917 in the National Army as Headquarters, 82nd Division

Organized 25 August 1917 at Camp Gordon, Georgia

Demobilized 27 May 1919 at Camp Mills, New York

Reconstituted 24 June 1921 in the Organized Reserves as Headquarters, 82nd Division

Organized 23 September 1921 at Columbia, South Carolina

Redesignated 13 February 1942 as Division Headquarters, 82nd Division

Ordered into active military service 25 March 1942 and reorganized at Camp Claiborne, Louisiana

Reorganized and redesignated 15 August 1942 as Headquarters, 82nd Airborne Division

Withdrawn 15 November 1948 from the Organized Reserve Corps and allotted to the Regular Army

Reorganized and redesignated 25 May 1964 as Headquarters and Headquarters Company, 82nd Airborne Division

CAMPAIGN PARTICIPATION CREDIT

World War I
Lorraine 1918
St. Mihiel
Meuse-Argonne

World War II
Sicily (only units in assault received arrowhead)
Naples-Foggia (Italy from the Sele River south of Salerno to the Volturno River)
Anzio (504th Combat Team units only)
Normandy (with arrowhead)
Rhineland (with arrowhead) (Holland)
Ardennes-Alsace (Battle of the Bulge)
Central Europe (Germany)

Armed Forces Expeditions
Dominican Republic
Grenada
Panama (with arrowhead)

Southwest Asia
Defense of Saudi Arabia (Operation DESERT SHIELD)
Liberation and Defense of Kuwait (Operation DESERT STORM)

Vietnam (3rd Brigade Only)
Tet Counteroffensive
Counteroffensive, Phase IV
Counteroffensive, Phase V
Counteroffensive, Phase VI
Tet 69/Counteroffensive
Summer-Fall 1969
Winter-Spring 1970

DECORATIONS

Presidential Unit Citation (Army), Streamer embroidered STE. MERE EGLISE
Meritorious Unit Commendation (Army), Streamer embroidered SOUTHWEST ASIA
French Croix de Guerre with Palm, WWII, Streamer embroidered STE. MERE EGLISE
French Croix de Guerre with Palm, WWII, Streamer embroidered COTENTIN
French Croix de Guerre, WWII, Fourragere
Belgian Fourragere 1940
Cited in the Order of the Day of the Belgian Army for actions in the Ardennes
Cited in the Order of the Day of the Belgian Army for action in Belgium and Germany
Military Oder of William (Degree of Knight of the Fourth Class), Streamer embroidered NIJMEGEN 1944
Netherlands Orange Lanyard

APPENDIX 2

The All American Soldier by SGT Carl Sigman

We're All American and proud to be
For we're the soldiers of liberty
Some ride the gliders through the enemy
Others are sky paratroopers
We're All American and fight we will
Till all the guns of the foe are stll
Airborne from skys of blue
We're coming through
Make your jumps
Take your bumps
Let's go!
Put on your boots
Your parachutes
Get all those gliders ready to attack today
For we'll be gone
Into the dawn
To fight 'em all the eighty-second way
Yes

APPENDIX 3

82nd Airborne Division
Medal of Honor Recipients

PIKE, EMORY J.

Rank and Organization: Lieutenant Colonel, Division Machine-gun Officer, 82nd Division. Place and Date: Near Vandieres, France, 15 September 1918. Entered Service at: Cuba. Citation: Having gone forward to reconnoiter new machine-gun positions, Colonel Pike offered his assistance in reorganizing advance infantry units which had become disorganized during a heavy artillery shelling. He succeeded in locating only about twenty men, but with these he advanced and when later joined by several infantry platoons rendered inestimable service in establishing outposts, encouraging all by his cheeriness, in spite of the extreme danger of the situation. When a shell had wounded one of the men in the outpost, Colonel Pike immediately went to his aid and was severely wounded himself when another shell burst in the same place. While waiting to be brought to the rear, Colonel Pike continued in command, still retaining his jovial manner of encouragement, directing the reorganization until the position could be held. The entire operation was carried on under terrific bombardment, and the example of courage and devotion to duty, as set by Colonel Pike, established the highest standard of morale and confidence to all under his charge. The wounds he received were the cause of his death.

YORK, ALVIN C.

Rank and Organization: Corporal, Company G, 328th Infantry, 82nd Division. Place and Date: Near Chatel-Chehery, France, 8 October 1918. Entered Service at: Pall Mall, Tennessee. Birth: Fentress County, Tennesee. G.O. No.: 59, W.D., 1919. Citation: After his platoon had suffered heavy casualties and three other noncommissioned officers had become casualties, Corporal York assumed command. Fearlessly leading seven men, he charged with great daring a machine-gun nest which was pouring deadly and incessant fire upon his platoon. In this heroic feat the machine-gun nest was taken, together with four officers and 128 men and several guns.

DEGLOPPER, CHARLES N.

Rank and Organization: Private First Class, Co. C, 325th Glider Infantry, 82nd Airborne Division. Place and Date: Mederet River at la Fiere, France, 9 June 1944. Entered Service at: Grand Island, New York. Birth: Grand Island, New York. G.O. No.: 22, 28 February 1946. Citation: He was a member of Company C, 325th Glider Infantry, on 9 June 1944 advancing with the forward platoon to secure a bridgehead across the Mederet River at la Fiere, France. At dawn the platoon had penetrated an outer line of machine guns and riflemen, but in so doing had become cut off from the rest of the company. Vastly superior forces began a decimation of the stricken unit and put in motion a flanking maneuver which would have completely exposed the American platoon in a shallow roadside ditch where it had taken cover. Detecting this danger, Private DeGlopper volunteered to support his comrades by fire from his automatic rifle while they attempted a withdrawal through a break in a hedgerow forty yards to the rear Scorning a concentration of enemy automatic weapons and rifle fire, he walked from the ditch onto the road in full view of the Germans. And sprayed the hostile positions with assault fire. He was wounded, but he continued firing. Struck again, he started to fall; and yet his grim determination and valiant fighting spirit could not be broken. Kneeling in the roadway, weakened by his grievous wounds, he leveled his heavy weapon against the enemy and fired burst after burst until killed outright. He was successful in drawing the enemy action away from his fellow soldiers, who continued the fight from a more advantageous position and established the first bridgehead over the Mederet. In the area where he made his intrepid stand his comrades later found the ground strewn with dead Germans and many machine guns and automatic weapons which he had knocked out of action. Private DeGlopper's gallant sacrifice and unflinching heroism while facing unsurmountable odds were in great measure responsible for a highly important tactical victory in the Normandy Campaign.

TOWLE, JOHN R.

Rank and Organization: Private, Company C, 504th Parachute Infantry, 82nd Airborne Division. Place and Date: Near Oosterhout, Holland, 21 September 1944. Entered Service at: Cleveland, Ohio. Birth: Cleveland, Ohio. G.O. No.:18, 15 March 1945. Citation: For conspicuous gallantry and intrepidity at the risk of his life above and beyond the call of duty on 21 September 1944, near Oosterhout, Holland. The rifle company in which Private Towle served as rocket launcher gunner was occupying a defensive position in the west sector of the recently established Nijmegen bridgehead when a strong enemy force of approximately 100 infantry supported by two tanks and a half-track formed for a counter attack. With full knowledge of the disastrous consequences resulting not only to his company but to the entire bridgehead by an enemy breakthrough, Private Towle immediately and without orders left his foxhole and moved 200 hundred yards in the face of intense small-arms fire to a position on an exposed dike roadbed. From this precarious position Private Towle fired his rocket launcher at and hit both tanks to his immediate front. Armored skirting on both tanks prevented penetration by the projectiles, but both vehicles withdrew slightly damaged. Still under intense fire and fully exposed to the enemy, Private Towle then engaged a nearby house which nine Germans had entered and were using as a strong point, and with one round killed all nine. Hurriedly replenishing his supply of ammunition, Private Towle, motivated only by his high conception of duty which called for the destruction of the enemy at any cost, then rushed approximately 125 yards through grazing fire to an exposed position from which he could engage the enemy half-track with his rocket launcher. While in a kneeling position preparatory to firing on the enemy vehicle, Private Towle was mortally wounded by a mortar shell. By his heroic tenacity, at the price of his life, Private Towle saved the lives of many of his comrades and was directly instrumental in breaking up the enemy counterattack.

FUNK, LEONARD A., JR.

Rank and Organization: First Sergeant, Company C, 508th Parachute Infantry, 82nd Airborne Division. Place and Date: Holzheim, Belgium, 29 January 1945. Entered Service at: Wilkinsburg, Pennsylvania. Birth: Braddock Township, Pennsylvania. G.O. No.75, 5 September 1945. Citation: He distinguished himself by gallant, intrepid actions against the enemy. After advancing fifteen miles in a driving snow storm, the American force prepared to attack through waist-deep drifts. The company executive officer became a casualty, and sergeant Funk immediately assumed his duties, forming headquarters soldiers into a combat unit for an assault in the face of direct artillery shelling and harassing fire from the right flank. Under his skillful and courageous leadership, this miscellaneous group and the Third Platoon attacked fifteen houses, cleared them and took thirty prisoners without suffering a casualty. The fierce drive of Company C quickly overran Holzheim, netting some eighty prisoners, who were placed under a four-man guard, all that could be spared, while the rest of the under-strength unit went about mopping up isolated points of resistance. An enemy patrol, by means of a ruse, succeeded in capturing the guards and freeing the prisoners, and had begun preparations to attack company C from the rear when Sergeant Funk walked around the building and into their midst. He was ordered to surrender by a German officer who pushed a machine-pistol into his stomach. Although overwhelmingly outnumbered and facing almost certain death, Sergeant Funk, pretending to comply with the order, began slowly to unsling his submachine from his shoulder and then, with lightning motion, brought the muzzle into line and riddled the German officer. He turned upon the other Germans, firing and shouting to the other Americans to seize the enemy's weapons. In the ensuing fight twenty-one Germans were killed, many wounded, and the remainder captured. Sergeant funk's bold action and heroic disregard for his own safety were directly responsible for the recapture of a vastly superior enemy force, which, if allowed to remain free, could have taken the widespread units of Company C by surprise and endangered the entire attack plan.

APPENDIX 4

Award of the Presidential Unit Citation

General Orders) War Department
No. 69) Washington 25, D.C., 22 August 1944

VIII.—BATTLE HONORS.-As authorized by Executive Order No. 9396 (sec. I Bull. 22, WD, 1943), superseding Executive Order No. 9075 (sec. III, Bull. 11 WD, 1942), citation of the following unit in General Orders No. 43 Headquarters 82d Airborne Division 4 August 1944, as approved by the Commanding General,, First United States Army, is confirmed under the provisions of section IV, Circular No. 333, War Department, 1943, in the name of the President of the United States as public evidence of deserved honor and distinction. The citation reads as follows:

Division Headquarters and Headquarters Company, 82d Airborne Division, is cited for outstanding performance of duty in action against the enemy between 6 and 9 June 1944 during the invasion of France. The Forward Echelon of Division Headquarters and Headquarters Company landed by parachute and glider on D-day, 6 June 1944, prior to H-hour, on the Cotentin Peninsula in the area surrounding Ste Mere Eglise, France. The enemy opposed drops and landings with intense antiairborne landing groups which attacked with machine guns, mortars, and artillery. Shortly after 0200, a division command post was established west of Ste Mere Eglise. Headquarters personnel were augmented by predawn glider elements landing about 0410, and by further gliderborne increments during the day. Headquarters personnel from many gliders, which had landed in areas not secured by parachute troops, fought their way to the Division Command Post, into which they infiltrated during the first 48 hours. The Division Staff and Headquarters and Headquarters Company labored without rest or relaxation day and night during the first 3 days of the invasion, at times under direct attack by artillery and small-arms fire, immediately adjacent to active fighting and frequently subjected to bombing attacks directed against its nearby artillery batteries. Duties were performed unhesitatingly with utter disregard for personal safety and with superior efficiency and tireless devotion to duty. The courage and perseverance shown by members of the Division Headquarters and Headquarters Company, 82d Airborne Division, are worthy of emulation and reflect the highest traditions of the Army of the United States.

The President of the Provisional Government of the French Republic cites the following units, being part of the 82nd Airborne Division...

They are authorized to carry the Fourragere in the colors of the Croix de Guerre, 1939-1945

APPENDIX 5

Award of the French Croix de Guerre and Fourragere of the Croix de Guerre, 1939-1945

Decision No. 159

The President of the Provisional Government of the French Republic: Cites in the Orders of the Army

Elite units of the 82nd Airborne Division which so magnificently distinguished themselves by parachuting into FRANCE during the night of 5 to 6 June 1944.

Through the military skill and heroism of their fighting men, they succeeded in seizing the important objective of Ste. Mere Eglise with very severe losses against stubborn resistance by the enemy, thus permitting the successful beach landing in force of the allied troops of liberation.

This citation carries the attribution of the Croix de Guerre with Palm.

Decision No. 160

The President of the Provisional Government of the French Republic: Cites in the Orders of the Army

These magnificent units, famed for their heroism and the spirit of sacrifice of their fighting men, gave further proof of their superior military quality in the course of the Battle of NORMANDY.

Comprising that part of the 82nd Airborne Division which had seized the roadlet and waterways commanding access to the landing beaches of the COTENTIN Peninsula, they sacrificed themselves without regard to the cost on the MEDERET and DOUVE Rivers, at SAINT-SAVEUR LE VICOMTE and ETIENNVILLE, from the 6th to the 20th of June 1944 in containing German reinforcements which were infinitely superior in numbers and firepower, forcing them to remain on the defensive and thus permit the arrival of the main force of he Allies.

This citation carries the attribution of the Croix de Guerre with Palm.

Decision No. 161

WHEREAS Decision No. 159 of 6 April 1946 attributes the Croix de Guerre with Palm to named units of the 82nd Airborne Division, and WHEREAS Decision No. 160 of 6 April 1946 attributes the Croix de Guerre with Palm to named units of the 82nd Airborne Division:

APPENDIX 6

Award of the Netherlands Military Order of William and Orange Lanyard (Degree of Knight of the Fourth Class)

Decree No. 30

Cited on 8 October 1945 by Wilhelmenia, Queen of the Netherlands, Princess of Orange-Nassau, with the following citation:

Considering that the 82nd Airborne Division of the United States Army, during the airborne operations and the ensuing fighting actions in the central part of the Netherlands in the period from 17 September to 4 October 1944, excelled in performing the tasks allotted to it, with tact, coupled with superior gallantry, self-sacrifice and loyalty; considering also, that the actions of the aforesaid division took place in the area of Nijmegen; have approved and ordered:

1. To decree that the divisional colors of the 82nd Airborne Division of the United States Army shall be decorated with the Military Order of William, degree of knight of the fourth class;
2. To authorize the division to carry in its divisional colors, the name of the town of NIJMEGEN 1944.

Decree No. 25

By decree of the Netherlands Minister of War, 8 October 1945, with the following citation:

Considering that the outstanding performance of duty of the 82nd Airborne Division, United States Army, during the airborne operations and ensuing fighting actions in the central part of the Netherlands in the period from 17 September to 4 October 1944, has induced HER MAJESTY, THE QUEEN, to decorate its divisional colors with the Military Order of William, degree of knight of the fourth class; considering also, that it is desirable for each member of the personnel of the 82nd Airborne Division, United States Army, who took part in the aforesaid operations, to possess a lasting memento of this glorious struggle; decrees: that each member of the personnel of the 82nd Airborne Division, United States Army, who took part in the operations in the area of Nijmegen in the period from 17 September to 4 October 1944 is allowed to wear the Orange Lanyard of the Royal Netherlands Army.

APPENDIX 7

Award of the Belgian Fourragere of the Croix de Guerre 1940-1945

Decree No. 1034
At the proposal of the Minister of National Defense, we have decreed and we order:

The 82nd Airborne Division with the 508th Parachute Infantry attached is cited twice in the Order of the Day for the Belgian Army and is herewith given the fourragere of 1940, for:

This elite Division which has gone with great elan through the campaigns of Tunisia, Sicily, Italy, Holland, and France, has distinguished itself particularly in the Battle of Ardennes from December 17 to December 31, 1944. Called upon as a reinforcement by the Allied High Command in the evening of the 17th of December, at a time when the Division was in the vicinity of Reims, the Division was able to take up combat positions in the region of Werbomont only 24 hours later and this under very severe climatic conditions. Progressing towards Ambleve and the Salm, the Division opened and maintained a corridor for the elements of four American divisions which were surrounded in the vicinity of St. Vith, thus giving new courage to the engaged units. The Division had prevented the enemy from piercing the north flank of the pocket created by the offensive of von Rundstedt and thus succeeded in saving the city of Liege and its surroundings from a second occupation by the Germans.

After having excelled in defensive warfare at the banks of the Salm and the Ambleve and after having repelled successfully the repeated attacks of the best German shock troops, the 82nd Airborne Division with the 508th Parachute Infantry attached, in spite of extreme cold and excessively deep snow, went on the offensive themselves, capturing 2500 German prisoners, including 5 battalion commanders. This fighting was extremely valorous as the organic composition of the division handicapped the unit considerably, not having at their disposal as any other infantry division would have, heavy weapons to support their attack. During 23 days, under most painful and adverse conditions, the veterans of the 82nd Airborne Division did not cease to give a wonderful example of courage and heroism, exemplifying their fighting spirit by several remarkably brilliant actions. By its valor, the Division wrote another page in heroic annals of Allied Airborne troops and rendered an important service to Belgium and to the Allied cause by establishing the necessary basis for the new pursuit of the enemy towards the Rhine River.

Index